THE OLD TESTAMENT

Fr Bede Rowe

THE OLD TESTAMENT

A theological understanding of the
Sacred Scriptures of the Catholic Church

Clamate voce maiore

Published in 2009
by Lulu.com
www.lulu.com

ISBN 978-1-4092-7402-5

Copyright Year: 2009
Copyright Notice: by Bede Rowe. All rights reserved.
The above information forms this copyright notice:
© *2009 by Bede Rowe. All rights reserved.*

This book is sold subject to the condition that is shall not, by way of trade or otherwise, be lent, resold, hired out, or otherwise circulated without the publisher's prior consent in any form of binding or cover other than that in which it is published and without a similar condition including this condition being imposed on a subsequent purchaser.

Dedicated
to
Fr Alexander Redman
and
Dr Francesca Stavrakopoulou

Contents

1	Introduction	9
2	What is the Bible?	15
3	The Canon of Sacred Scripture	25
4	The Interpretation of Sacred Scripture	35
5	The Revelation of God	43
6	The Sources of the Old Testament	51
7	History	57
8	Myth and Legend	105
9	Prophecy	131
10	Wisdom	153
11	Law	175
12	Psalms and Worship	193
13	Apocalypse and the Coming of Christ	215
14	Afterword	239

Appendix A:	The Council of Trent	243
Appendix B:	Divino Afflante Spiritu	247
Appendix C:	Dei Verbum	253
Appendix D:	Interpretation of Biblical Texts	259

1
INTRODUCTION

Throughout her history the Church has had to battle against ideas or positions which are contrary to the truth which has been revealed to her. We can see this in the great conflicts which surrounded the development of the doctrines of the nature of Christ. Was He just an inspired prophet of God, chosen and anointed but fundamentally a man like you and me, or was He God Himself who took on a human cloak so that He could walk about among His creation?

In the early Church both of these views had proponents and the arguments that went back and forth were long and drawn out, even sometimes to the point of physical violence. The Church, seeing the truth that had come to her through the Sacred Scriptures, and also the truth that was hers through her Tradition, accepted neither of these views and condemned them both. She did this not because she wanted to stifle free expression or because she was a terrible mother who refused to allow her children to think for themselves, but rather because it was her duty to help her members, Christians throughout the ages, to win salvation and come to the glories of heaven.

Introduction

In this she had been given a knowledge of the truth which was not just hers to be kept and guarded but was for the whole world, and as such was to be proclaimed to all times and in all places. If she ignored this knowledge of the truth then she would not be fulfilling her role as the Bride of Christ. What mother would allow her children to believe things that would be harmful to them?

This may seem a strange way to begin thinking about the Old Testament but in reality it is not. In the early second century there arose a school of thought under the name of the theologian Marcion. His views of the Old Testament came from a society in which there were many groups of people with beliefs which incorporated elements of the religions around them. One thing that many of them had in common was the peddling of secret knowledge. These groups claimed to offer salvation, but their knowledge came at a price. The price was being part of the group, often with other strings attached. As they held the way to salvation, as they falsely thought, their name comes to us from the Greek term *gnosis*, γνωσις, meaning knowledge. They are the Gnostics.

As is the case in a market in which there are many sellers and a limited number of buyers, they had to make their product attractive and distinctive. It was attractive because it gave the buyer the chance of heaven, and each group, more or less, stressed exclusive elements in their beliefs. Some were influenced by the Egyptian gods and goddesses. Others were closer to various Roman mystery cults. What we identify as Marcionism was very close to mainstream Christianity, but with one major difference. This was his view of the Old Testament, and more specifically the God of the Old Testament.

A general feature of the Gnostics was that they were not too fond of the material world. This is a danger that we find in Christianity throughout her history - a rejection of the physical world in favour of the spiritual. Perhaps in our day we can see its shadow in the thought that runs, "it's not what you do, it's what you feel".

The Gnostics, and Marcion in particular, held a similar view to this division between the material and the spiritual. They knew that the Old Testament contained accounts of the creation of the world by God, but they could not reconcile this God with the God of the New Testament. The latter seemed to bring spiritual salvation while the former was much more concerned with the mess and violence of life. How on the one hand could Our Saviour preach peace and the turning of the other cheek, while on the other hand the Old Testament spoke of devastation and destruction explicitly at the command of God? We need only to look at what happened to the world at the time of the flood for an example of this. The God of the New Testament preached forgiveness seventy times seven, while the God of the Old Testament wiped out all mankind, except eight chosen ones. Exactly how great a crime must the world have committed to justify such a response?

While contemplating these things, Marcion and others connected them with their view that the material world was somehow tainted. They came up with a radical yet logical conclusion: the two Gods were different. The God of the Old Testament, bound up with creating the world and acting in a manner which reflects our baser side, was different from the God of the New Testament whom Christ had come to proclaim. They were not the same, and as the New Testament was concerned with the spirit, then the God of the New Testament was infinitely superior to the God of the Old Testament.

What then happened to the Old Testament Scriptures which tell us about this vengeful and wrathful God? At the very least they were downplayed, and indeed usually they were discarded. They did not give a picture of God that was compatible with the Gnostic's world view.

Put bluntly what we called Marcionism called for Christianity to be cut away from the Sacred Hebrew scriptures and all that they contained. They were not good for salvation and the God who they talked about had nothing, or very, very little, to do with the revelation of Jesus Christ. It is also worth mentioning that Marcion was not terribly fond of huge sections of the New Testament either. Indeed the only Gospel that he approved of was St John. Not only did the entire Old Testament find itself excluded, so did Saints Matthew, Mark and Luke!

And so the Church condemned him along with the whole way of thinking that brought about any diminishment of the Old Testament and the physical world. She recognised that these Scriptures were the ones which had nurtured and sustained Our Lord as He grew up in His family. It was the Passover as described in the Old Testament that His foster father St Joseph would have presided over, and more importantly, it was the prophetic witness and the apocalyptic vision which had been given through the chosen people of God that He was to fulfil and surpass.

If you cut away the Old Testament, then you cut away the roots of Christ Himself.

For all its difficulties, and complexities, for all the arguments of interpretation and subsequent heresies and spurious theologies to which the distortion of the Old Testament gave rise, still we are welded to it as surely as we are welded to our parents and ancestors. We cannot re-write our history as if God had made a mistake.

The challenge is now, as it has always been, the correct interpretation of Holy Scripture. Simply eradicating it because we find it difficult or perplexing is not an option. We knew that in the second century and we know it now.

This then is the reason why we study the Old Testament and find therein the seeds of the coming of Christ and the nourishment of our own faith. We hope that this book will help to some degree in this great endeavour.

Introduction

An image from Codex Sinaiticus. It is one of two copies of the Septuagint. It is called Sinaiticus as it was kept for many years at St Catherine's Monastery at the foot of Mount Sinai. It is handwritten in Greek script.

2

WHAT IS THE BIBLE?

We take it for granted that we have the Bible. The term itself comes from the Greek βιβλος meaning book. This also, however, raises problems. Where did this book come from? When did we get it? Who decided which parts were to be included? Was there any choice?

The first stage of our definition is to state what we do not believe. We do not believe that the Bible was given to us by Divine intervention which did not involve the active agency of human beings. Other faith systems have this high view of inerrancy in their holy books, for example the Muslim faith and the Quran. They believe that an angel came and dictated it to Mohammed. He did the angel's bidding and thus the words, the very text of the Quran, is thought to be of divine, not human, origin. Their belief cuts out the human element. This is why for them the argument will always centre on the interpretation of the text, and not the text itself.

This view of the Bible has never been part of the Church's view of her Sacred Scriptures. That is not to say that such a view of the Bible has never existed, or indeed does not exist now. We could go so far as to say that one of the major challenges to belief in Christianity at the moment comes directly from this un-Catholic view of her sacred texts. Indeed one of the threats within Catholicism has been an incorporation of a fundamentally incorrect view of Sacred Scripture.

For want of a better term let us call this view of Sacred Scripture "Biblicism". It places the texts of the Bible almost on a par with the texts briefly described above concerning the Islamic faith. It affords an "inerrancy" - that is that it is free not only from theological error, but also from every other kind of error - to the Bible in general and, for our purposes, the Old Testament in particular. The plain reading is seen to be revealed by God and thus has to be believed for our salvation. With regard to the Old Testament this often had the meaning of the revelation of historic truth.

How did this view come about? It is the direct opposite of Marcion's which we have already mentioned, but it falls into the same trap. It provides an unnuanced and easy view of faith. Marcion vaunted a secret knowledge; the Biblicists do exactly the same thing. By elevating Sacred Scripture to the position of the touchstone of salvation and investing it with an inerrancy guaranteed by God, they find their own way to heaven. All you need to do is to accept the Bible and to live by it, and heaven is yours. As can easily be seen, the issue concerns neither an argument from the text, nor indeed with explicit revelations from God, but rather with a need for authority.

As we have just mentioned, there is a constant temptation towards this view of the Scriptures throughout the history of the

Church, but the rise of this type of Biblicism can be traced to the time of the Reformation. By the term 'Reformation' we mean the political and theological turmoil of the sixteenth and seventeenth centuries which gave rise to communities of Christians who existed and worshipped in the West outside the Catholic Church. They rebelled against and explicitly rejected Catholic teaching. What follows is painted with pretty broad brushstrokes as we are not providing a history of the time of the Reformation, but trying to understand how an elevation of the position of Sacred Scripture occurred.

The central issue in the Reformation was authority. More than anything else it was a rebellion of certain peoples and nations against the control and power of the Catholic Church. Of course within it there were individuals who were compelled by what they thought were genuine religious motives, but the result was a crisis of authority.

In the West since the earliest times, there had been a clear appreciation of where the power of salvation lay. It was firmly in the institution of the Church and the practice of her rites. It was through her that the priests had the authority and power to take away sins and offer the sacrifice of the Mass, not only for the good of the living, but also for the relief of the dead. This authority was mediated directly from Christ Himself through the choice and institution of St Peter and the Papacy. It continued through the ages and resided in the traditions and practices of the Church, governed and ruled by St Peter's successors. After all, who else had the power to excommunicate and cast outside the visible bounds of salvation, if not the one to whom the keys of the Kingdom had been given?

When the rebellion against the Church took place a major problem remained. The rebellion had found a fertile soil in nations and in princes who wanted to exercise their own authority and power over their subjects, in matters not just of the flesh but in matters of the spirit as well. The communities of Christians which came about as a result of this process could physically survive if they were protected by their prince, but how could they survive theologically? What gave their ministers authority? How did they know that what they were doing was correct? What moral guidance could they follow? All of this had been provided by the edifice of the Church. When they no longer accepted the authority of the Church, what else could be put in its place? The answer was the one thing that they had left once the practice of the faith had been radically altered and the timeless truths that they and their ancestors had been taught were now proclaimed as not only wrong, but leading to damnation.

This one thing was the Bible.

It became the touchstone of authority. If something was not explicitly attested to in the Bible, then it was not to take place in these new communities of believers. As an example of this, there was the rise of a group of believers called Anabaptists who rejected infant baptism. They said that such a practice was not found written in the pages of the Bible. Also, the practice of praying for the dead, which was one of the first and greatest marks of Christianity, was cast aside. This was done not because of

The Old Testament

Sacred Scripture, but rather for social and political reasons. The supreme prayer for the dead was the sacrifice of the Mass, but this was in the power of the priests, whose authority came from the Church. To cut away that authority, you had to get rid of the sacrificing priests, and the easiest and best way was to attack what they were most readily identified with, namely the celebration of the Sacrifice. The common people, of course, found this most disturbing. They knew that they had a deep seated desire within them to help, by their prayers and actions, the souls of their beloved dead. To cut away the authority of the Church was to cut away the need for the Church, and this could only be done by a kind of theological engineering. Those who suffered were the people who were left with no way to help their deceased families and friends.

The scalpel that was used was the Bible itself. You could state that the sacrifice had been offered once by Christ on the cross. You could further say that there was no description of the Mass in the Bible as the people had seen it offered day after day, but there remained the rather sticky problem that the Bible did not actually do what these reformers wanted; it did not say what they wanted it to say. This is not in itself surprising as the Bible, being of God, could not be placed in conflict the Church which He Himself had founded. The Bible, in the pages of the Second Book of the Maccabees not only commented on praying for the dead, but described it as a good and laudable thing to do. Speaking of Judas Maccabeus it says:

> For if he were not expecting that those who had fallen would rise again, it would have been superfluous and foolish to pray for the dead. But if he was looking to the splendid reward that is laid up for those who fall asleep in godliness, it was a holy and pious thought. Therefore he made atonement for the dead that they might be delivered from their sin.
>
> II Maccabees 12:44-45

The answer that came to the reformers was at once simple and radical.

They cut it out. They eradicated I and II Maccabees, Tobit, Judith, Wisdom, Ecclesiasticus and Baruch as well as sections of Esther and various parts of the prophet Daniel.

They excised the sections of the Bible that did not agree with their theology. Once this had been done it became increasingly easy to continue. At one point Martin Luther dismissed many parts not only of the Old Testament, but also the letter of St James and large tracts of the Gospels themselves. Sacred Scripture did not fit in with the new theology so Sacred Scripture was changed.

Quite rightly you may well ask if this is not in direct conflict with the Biblicist view of the Bible as outlined above. Of course it is, but there was no other option open. There was no other tangible place where authority could lie. The fact that the Bible had to be altered (although the final alterations were not as extreme as Luther had proposed) and books excised, and a rigid form of interpretation imposed, did not lessen the fact that this work, never designed for such a role, and quite contrary to the fundamental principles of Christianity, was elevated to the heights and given the power of the Papacy. Its authority until quite recently was as rigidly imposed as the most extreme form of Papal obedience.

Biblicism then is the elevation of the authority of Sacred Scripture to include inerrancy in all matters not only with regards to faith, but also to other concerns that Scripture addresses. After all, since Scripture itself makes no division between history, creation, moral law, example and custom, who has the power, the authority to interpret or curtail it? Who is to say if the book of Jonah is a historical work or not? Did he actually travel to Nineveh or is it an allegorical story?

In our own time Biblicism has two broad forms. The first is a Biblical fundamentalism, which proclaims that everything within Sacred Scripture is correct in every part and detail. Creationists who insist on the exact manner of creation as found in the first chapters of the book of Genesis are an example of this view. The second form is Biblical liberalism which holds that the Bible is the source par excellence which holds the way to salvation, but does not necessarily believe that historical or abiding truth is found within it.

It is quite easy to identify both theologies in Christianity.

It was stated above that these views are a challenge to Christianity in general and the Catholic Church in particular. Let us explore that for a moment. The general challenge to Christianity is that Biblical fundamentalism is ascribed to the belief of Christians with no differentiation: all believers are assumed to believe the same thing. Anything, then, that comes along and challenges this fundamentalist view challenges faith as a whole. Often we see this with regard to the issue of creation. Broadly speaking if an individual is a Christian, then they will be tarred with the brush that says "you are anti science, because science has disproven the account of creation found in the Bible. If you cannot be trusted to believe science, then not only is your faith based on nonsense, but also you as an individual are intellectually bankrupt". The argument for or against God is clouded by issues which have nothing to do with the fundamental propositions of our faith. It is almost as if in the eyes of the non believer fundamentalism cannot be separated from Christianity.

Science and faith have been pitted against each other, and quite frankly, it is science which gets electricity into our homes, and develops medicines which heal our bodies. It is science which puts aeroplanes in the sky and investigates the extremities of space. Pitted one against the other, what little boy or girl would not prefer playing with dinosaurs and imagining them going on a rampage to being told that they never existed and are just made-up animals?

With relation to the Catholic Church in particular, Biblicism, of either form, has crept into our faith and sometimes occupies a place which itself should not exist. Biblicism has no place in orthodox Catholicism. The Bible, of course, does have a distinct and honoured place, but only when yoked together with Tradition and the Magisterium of the Church. If ever Catholicism moves away from this threefold strand then imbalance enters and heresy flourishes. Catholicism has no need to defend herself from challenges such as "but where does it say that in the Bible?" for such a question is nonsense. It only has meaning if you believe that authority resides in something other than the Church.

"Where is the Immaculate Conception of Our Lady mentioned in the New Testament? What about her Assumption into heaven? What about the practice of Indulgences? Where are the Pope, the Bishops and the hierarchical nature of the Church in the pages of Sacred Scripture?" These are only valid questions if one has a Biblicist view of the sacred text. To Catholics, although they are often challenged with such questions by non-Catholics, the questions themselves are meaningless.

To use a homely example and to describe the interplay between Scripture, Magisterium and Tradition, suppose an official biography of a famous man were to be written, and everything within was a straightforward statement of fact. What would be the place of the personal memories of those who had known him when he was a boy? They are true, but they are not contained in the official biography. Were one to ignore them, even though they came from his mother, father, family and friends, would the view of the man be increased or diminished? Of course, such memories exist and are cherished. Such is the Catholic view of Tradition. It is not in conflict with the official factual biography, but rather is an important aspect of a witness to the truth. The purpose of the Magisterium, in Catholic thought, is to be the authority which says that this version of the biography is correct; the facts do not deceive. It is also the same authority which says this tradition is valid because this or that person is true and honest; the memories are not false.

This is not meant to be a *tour de force* or apologetic for the theology and self understanding of the Catholic Church, but it is impossible to look at the Old Testament without first having boundaries in place and rules for interpretation. These are found in the traditions and teaching of the Church throughout the ages.

3

The Canon of Sacred Scripture

Having addressed the authority of Sacred Scripture, we need for a moment to look at the Old Testament itself and more specifically, its composition. As mentioned above, the Bible did not arrive in our laps as a completed from God or His angels. What we will do in the main body of this work is look at different types of literature in the Bible to see, if we can, what they show us about our faith and the faith of those who composed them.

In looking at the Old Testament, however, we have to decide what texts we are to look at in the first place. The 'Canon' is the term used for the books which are included in any given work. It comes from the Greek term κανων meaning 'rule' or 'that which grows straight'.

Often we simply take it for granted that there is an Old Testament and that you can find it by looking at the first part of the Bible. If you take a look at any religion section in a reputable book shop, you will soon find that things are not so easy. Of course there is a plethora of different Bibles, in different translations intended for different audiences. Because of this it is almost impossible to provide a translation which is free from bias.

A particular translator makes a choice in using one word rather than another. This choice is informed by his background, intended audience and theological point of view. If you are unfortunate enough to pick up a Street Bible then you would be wise to put it down very quickly. Perhaps it is attractive and accessible to its intended audience but equally it may be just a condescending gimmick. Of course there is value in children's Bibles, as their level of understanding is less developed that that of an adult, and at one level, this follows the practice of telling Bible stories in stained glass windows that we find in old churches.

Concerning the specific practice of translation, however, let us take the example of the following section from the first letter to Timothy, chapter 3. The first few verses read:

> If any one aspires to the office of bishop, he desires a noble task. Now a bishop must be above reproach, the husband of one wife, temperate, sensible, dignified, hospitable, an apt teacher, no drunkard, not violent but gentle, not quarrelsome, and no lover of money.

The word referred to above in the Revised Standard Version translation is 'bishop'; in Greek επισκοπη. It is from this root that the Latin term *episcopus* comes - the usual word for a Bishop. This has been part of the traditional defence of the hierarchical structure of the Church. If someone wishes to cut away the position of the Bishop, then the easiest thing to do is to re-translate επισκοπη as "overseer". This does not have the same hierarchical connotations. The base text, of course, remains the same, but the translation has put a theological gloss on the text. The International Standard Version, The New American Standard Version and the World English Bible are just some translations which have gone down the "overseer", "elder" route. If your Christian group does not accept the existence of bishops as an authoritative expression of your particular church community, then there will be a great temptation to get rid of such a term whenever it occurs in the Bible.

In what follows we will use the original Revised Standard Version of the Bible. The numbering system for the Psalms is Greek and is found on page 194.

It is not just the translation that is different; it is the very books themselves that are included for translation. The main differences stem from whether or not they are Catholic Bibles. It is easier to say Catholic and non-Catholic Bibles, as all of the non-Catholic Bibles agree on omitting some of the Books in the Old Testament, but they do not all originate from one single tradition dating from the time of the Reformation.

To understand how this came about we have to begin a few centuries before Christ.

We must assume that the texts of the Sacred Scriptures existed to a large degree in the language of the people who composed or compiled them. This would, of course, have been Hebrew. We have to be careful here, however, for we know that when the Books of the Law were read out in the book of Nehemiah, they were not only proclaimed but also translated, for the people had forgotten the very language of the Scriptures:

> And they read from the book, from the law of God, clearly; and they gave the sense, so that the people understood the reading.
>
> Nehemiah 8:8

This seemingly little aside in history is quite important, because by it we can see that the People of God were not Hebrew speakers to the exclusion of all other languages. Even though we can assume that Sacred texts preserve a purity of language which is not dependent upon the common people, it does not in and of itself exclude the use of other languages.

As the Jewish people spread through the world and a working knowledge of Hebrew waned, it was replaced by Aramaic in the Holy Land and by Ancient Greek throughout the land around the Mediterranean. To a large extent this can be traced back to the time of Alexander the Great in the mid fourth century BC.

One century after Alexander in the middle of the third century BC, the Jewish Scriptures were systematically translated into the common language, Greek. This process probably began with the *Torah*, that is the Books of the Law (Genesis, Exodus, Leviticus, Numbers, and Deuteronomy). In the following centuries the other Hebrew Sacred texts were likewise translated. Together they are given the name the 'Septuagint' (LXX). This term comes from the Latin title *septuaginta interpretum versio*, "the translation of the seventy interpreters". The Septuagint was believed to have been the work of seventy scholars who worked on the texts and produced the final translation. Many legends grew up surrounding

The Old Testament

the production of the Septuagint. In the Letter of Aristeas, seventy two scholars were involved (six from each of the twelve tribes). They had been asked by the King of Egypt, Ptolemy II Philadelphus, to translate the Scriptures into Greek so that they could be included in the great library in Alexandria. These seventy two men were locked up in separate rooms and worked away on their translations. When they had all finished and the versions compared they were all found to be miraculously the same. Just for good measure, they were also supposed to have completed their task in seventy two days.

Of course we are not bound to believe the traditional story about the production of the Septuagint, but what it shows us is that a Greek version of the Hebrew Scriptures was produced in the time of Ptolemy II Philadelphus and that its production was thought to be the work of divine intervention.

If we stop at this point in history, then we have a translation, the Septuagint, and something from which it was translated, namely the original texts. We do not know if this original set of texts was wholly written in Hebrew, or whether they contained other languages. All we do know for certain is that, as a body of work, the translation known as the Septuagint existed.

This becomes increasingly important because of the spread of Christianity. The Septuagint had more or less taken the place of Hebrew texts in Jewish worship and in common Jewish knowledge. When the Scriptures are referred to in the New Testament, it is the Septuagint that is meant. When quotations are made, they are from the Septuagint, and it would not be too much to say that for the vast majority of the Jewish people, their Sacred Scriptures only existed in Greek and most definitely could only be understood in Greek.

This caused no problem until Christianity arrived and used the Jewish Scriptures to understand the person of Jesus Christ, His mission and His purpose. As Christianity spread, more people encountered the Old Testament. However their understanding of the Hebrew Scriptures was based on the Christian interpretation of the sacred text. To counter this threat to their Scriptures the Jews, some of whom had relocated to the town of Jamnia, began to consider the problem of the identification of the Septuagint with Christianity. They decided that the Septuagint would no longer be used in worship and that only Hebrew texts could be studied and read. This was not a sudden decision but rather a process, and took place between the years 70AD and 135AD. As they scoured their scrolls any Greek elements within them were cast out and only Hebrew was retained. Indeed the Jews at this council also included books which did not exist in the Septuagint, such as Enoch and the book of Jubilees, and excluded some which did exist in Hebrew, such as the Books of the Maccabees. St Jerome had copies of the latter in Hebrew, though they were subsequently lost.

Within Christian circles the next stage came with the same St Jerome (mid fourth century AD). St Jerome was working on a translation of the Bible into Latin. This became known as the Vulgate. To do this he used a number of versions. These included not only the Septuagint, but also the Hebrew texts, which of course differed from the Septuagint as all non-Hebrew sections had removed. St Jerome was of the opinion that the base text which should be used for translation was the Hebrew and not the Septuagint. He therefore wanted to limit the books of the Old Testament to the texts which the Jews used. The Septuagint had 46 books, the Hebrew only 39. He wished to leave out the Books of Tobit, Judith, I and II Maccabees, the Wisdom of Solomon, Ecclesiasticus and Baruch. It is thanks to St Jerome that we have the term Apocrypha. This was the name that he gave to these seven books, a name which means 'hidden'. Of course in common language now it has come to mean something that is old, and which generally is not true. This was not St Jerome's original meaning.

To leave out these books may have been St Jerome's scholarly opinion, but it was not the opinion of the Church, and so the Vulgate was authorised to contain all of the books found in the Septuagint, and moreover, the books in their entirety. When the Jews had excised all non Hebrew elements of their Sacred Scriptures they had removed not only whole books but also passages within works for which they only had versions in Greek, such as sections of the Prophet Daniel.

Why is this important?

We saw above that during the Reformation the Bible was given an exalted status, and moreover was open to being changed for theological reasons. The reformers decided that the Bible should only contain the elements which existed in Hebrew. They followed the logic of St Jerome (who in turn, of course, was following the anti-Christian decision of the Jews to restrict their texts to Hebrew to preserve them from the Christian Church). In part the reformers' justification was also the new learning coming to the fore in northern Europe. This looked back at original texts, and through study increased access to the ancient languages. Hebrew was the prized language.

The result was that they cut out the seven books, even though they existed before Christ at least in Greek and in some cases in Hebrew as well (such as the Books of the Maccabees). As well as whole books, they also excised individual sections of the Old Testament which could only be found in their third century BC Greek translation.

From this brief historical overview we can see that even the text of the Bible which is used is a polemical choice.

What physical texts do we now have at our disposal? The most ancient full manuscripts that we possess date from the fourth century AD. These are the Greek texts of the Septuagint, called *Codex Vaticanus* and *Codex Sinaiticus*. Next are fifth century texts in Syriac, called the *Peshitta*, and in Latin, called the Vulgate. The oldest Hebrew text dates from five hundred years later, from the tenth century, the Masoretic text called *Codex Leningradensis*.

From this it would seem that if you want to find the oldest texts of the Old Testament then you are forced to use the Greek Septuagint, then Syriac and Latin, followed by Hebrew.

All of this changed in 1947 when a shepherd boy broke some clay jars in a cave in Qumran and discovered the Dead Sea Scrolls. These texts, dating from one hundred and fifty BC to seventy AD are by far the oldest extant texts of the Old Testament.

What is surprising to some, however, is that when they were examined they did not agree with the tenth century Masoretic text, but rather with the Greek text of the Septuagint. It could not be claimed, as some in the past had, that the Catholic Scriptures were based on a bad Greek translation of books some of which were not even found in the pristine Hebrew Old Testament.

Our Canon of Scripture, then, was simply fixed by the seventy scholars who began the process of translation of the Hebrew Scriptures into Greek in Alexandria some years before the coming of Christ. They were used and accepted by Our Saviour and hallowed by the Church.

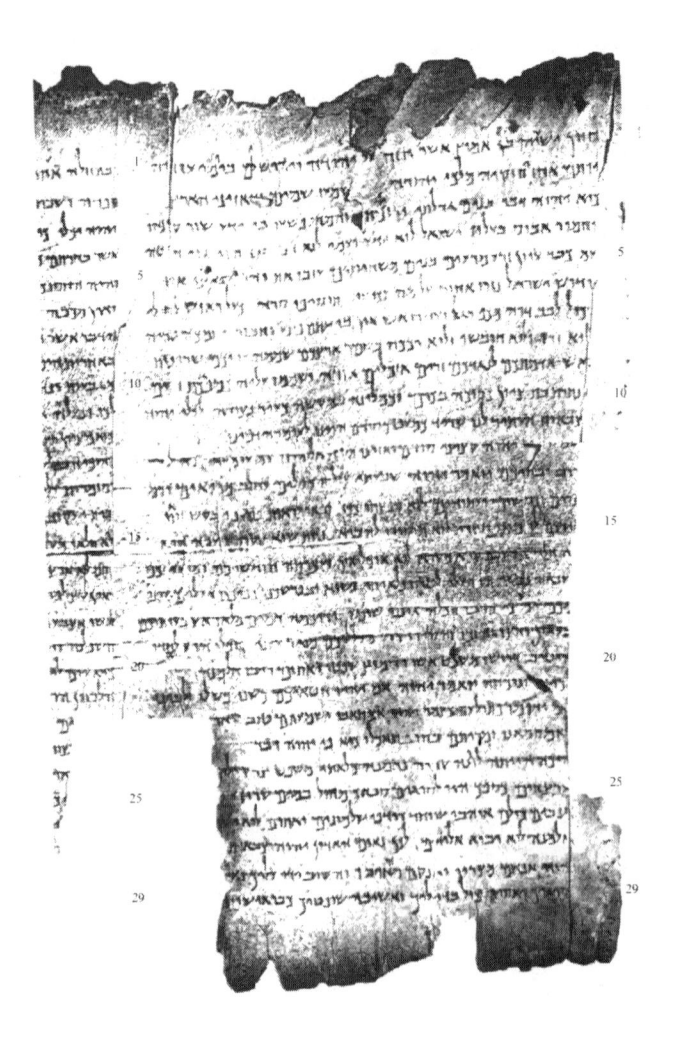

*A section from the Book of the Prophet Isaiah found at Qumran. These scrolls are the oldest Hebrew versions of the Old Testament.
In many places the language and phraseology agree with the Septuagint rather than the later Masoretic Text.*

4

The Interpretation of Sacred Scripture

Having looked at the composition of the Old Testament and some of the questions surrounding which books are included, we have to decide how we are going to look not only at the texts themselves, but also at the Old Testament as a whole.

There are various methods which theologians have developed over the years to help in this task. It is often thought that Old Testament criticism and interpretation did not really begin until the rise of certain German theologians in the nineteenth century. Indeed we have to acknowledge that they pushed Biblical studies to the fore and used tools which were new and novel. Biblical interpretation, however, had an honourable lineage long before that time.

In the works of Origen of Alexandria (185-254AD) we see a multi-level method of interpretation. One layer was the plain meaning of the text. What does the text say and what does it mean? Another is an allegorical meaning. What does the text mean to the human condition? A further level is the spiritual meaning and finally the typological meaning. Typology is no longer really used in academic theology, but is of great importance if only for the reason that we see it being employed in the New Testament itself. "And as Moses lifted up the serpent in the wilderness, so must the Son of man be lifted up" (John 3:14).

If anything, Biblical criticism has developed the first of these layers of interpretation and left the others to a different branch of theology, a branch which is more to do with faith, and less to do with academics.

Academic criticism moved through various phases and stressed various elements at different times. Most of these do not concern us. However, the search for what the text means can be divided into two. Classically these are called Higher and Lower Criticism. Lower Criticism is concerned with the words of the text themselves. It looks at the passage with which it is presented and tries to understand the bare bones of what it says.

This may seem a little odd to us, but if we look at the arguments about what text is used in the first place, then we can see that Lower Criticism is not straightforward. Most Biblical criticism uses the Masoretic Text. This text was copied between the seventh and tenth centuries by a group of Jews called the Masoretes. It is both a consonantal and vocalised text. Although the Masoretes were very faithful to what has been handed on to them, the texts themselves are corrupt. Put quite simply, in some places we do not know what the words mean. Either the meanings of the words have been lost, or the letters of the text are incorrect. In Ecclesiastes 12:5 there is a word which can be variously translated. The word in Hebrew is הָאֲבִיּוֹנָה, and is translated as a caper-berry, a caper bush, almond tree or desire. It is the only instance of it in the Old Testament. Its meaning is closed off from us.

Lower Criticism will try to discover a translation of the word. It will look at parallel places where the consonantal text is used and see if there are any clues that can be gathered from that context. It may look at other places outside the Biblical Canon to see if that is any clearer. It will look at various translations, notably, though not exclusively, the Septuagint.

This may seem of little importance. After all what does it matter if a particular word can have two or more meanings? For us this is important because it shows yet again that the text of the Bible is not the divinely written work that some would have us believe. What is the point of God dictating words, if we do not know the meaning of those words?

Higher Criticism does something different. It looks at texts as a whole and tries to see what they mean. What would they have meant to the people who wrote or spoke them? What would they have meant to those who would have received them? Can we see different texts having been joined together at some point? Are there different strands within a text which can be delineated? What does a text mean in the form and style in which it was written?

It is this latter tool that we will use to gain a better understanding of the Old Testament. In the sections below we will look at different types of literature within the Bible. We will examine where they came from, what forms they take, and the truth that they are trying to convey. In this way we can attempt to see the development of the religion of the people of the Old Testament.

Even in the literature of our own time we can see something similar happening. If we look at "The charge of the Light Brigade" by Alfred, Lord Tennyson we know that it was written in 1854 just a few months after the event. What this poetry does is something different from a historical account, giving dates and names and the like. It is true in the sense that it conveys much more accessibly the reality of being in the middle of a cavalry charge. We know that it is the 'Valley of Death' because of what subsequently happened there. Is it less true because some details may not be historically accurate, or because the facts that are correct are relayed in a particular poetical style? If the poem were claiming to be a history text book that charge could be levelled at it. However, it performs a very different function. This is not to say that it cannot be used to look at what happened when the Light Brigade charged. It may have had at its disposal first hand accounts, or oral history which is no longer available to us. We know this charge was into the 'Valley of Death', while geographically it was into the valley between the Fedyukhin Heights and the Causeway Heights. It is Tennyson's description, however, that one remembers.

If we wish to parallel this with something in the Old Testament, then we can consider the account of Moses leading the People of Israel through the Red Sea in the historical work of Exodus 14 and in Psalm 134 and 135.

Both of these testify to the same historical event but do so in very different ways.

By looking at the various types of literature in the Old Testament, we are honouring the integrity of the Bible itself. Very little, if any, would now be classified as an objective historical recording of fact. Even the lists of Kings and the collections of laws may have been influenced by political machinations.

We have to keep in mind that the Old Testament is not one work divided into chapters and books, but rather is a collection of books, as if it were a kind of library. In a library there are various different sections: Romance, History, Poetry, DVDs containing music and songs, Fantasy and the like. Similarly in the Old Testament there are sections and subsections.

We will look at the following sections: History, Myth and Legend, Prophecy, Law, Wisdom, Psalms and Worship and finally Apocalyptic Literature. Of course there are obvious books which neatly fall into one or other category. The Book of the Psalms falls into Psalms and Worship. Proverbs falls into Wisdom Literature. History is found in I and II Samuel, I and II Kings and I and II Chronicles, Ezra and Nehemiah and finally the works of the Maccabees. There is, however, also a great overlap. Some accounts of worship are found in historical works and the prophets. Myth and Legend is found throughout the Old Testament.

In looking at types of literature, we will cross over the divisions of individual works and texts and take the witness of the Old Testament as a whole.

If this collection of Sacred Scriptures is of God (though not dictated by Him) then we can understand it in a greater depth if we seek answers and knowledge from the entirety of the work.

This way of looking at the Old Testament falls into the Higher Criticism section called 'Form Criticism' as it looks at the forms or types of literature. We will also use a tool called Source Criticism which looks at various parts of a text and sees whether they originally belonged together or whether they were joined together at some subsequent point for a particular reason.

Very broadly this may be outlined as follows. Different works in the Old Testament came about in different ways. Songs would first have been sung for many years and handed down orally before being written down. Ancient stories would have been part of the oral history, recited, almost chanted, without change or deviation from the dark mists of time. They may well have owed more to Ancient Near Eastern tales than anything specifically Israelite. Prophets wrote down little but their prophetic utterances may have been recorded by others in guilds or by their companions. When history came to be written, it was done so not to show necessarily what historically happened, but what God was doing, how He was acting and manifesting His power in any specific situation. The truth lay in what the history affirmed.

Source Criticism also supposes that when particular groups gained access to various texts and works they readily changed small sections, or placed certain parts side by side, to alter the emphasis or meaning subtly. It is not a whole scale re-writing, but rather a marshalling of facts to emphasise a point. To some extent we ourselves often do this in our everyday lives.

The work itself is from one particular standpoint, and the bias within it betrays that fact. This is the meaning of another type of criticism, or way of looking at the Old Testament, known as 'Redaction Criticism'. It is a process of editing or marshalling facts for a particular purpose or intention. It is a deliberate process, but not one of falsification. The intention is not to give an untrue version of events, but rather one which is more true for it gives an explicit meaning to what happened. This may be as insignificant as wishing to remember a specific name or place. It may be as important as ignoring the reigns of particular Kings and trying to airbrush them from history.

If we look at examples in our world we frequently see the process of this revisionist history taking place, from the re-writing of the slave trade, to the involvement of particular countries in various wars.

The interpretation of Sacred Scripture has to take into account all these things so that we can see not just what an original writer may have thought and said, but also what each of the layers of meaning intended. This enriches and deepens the mystery of the Old Testament's fundamental purpose.

That purpose is the preparation of the world through the People of God for the coming of God Himself in the flesh, and the salvation brought to us through Our Lord and Saviour Jesus Christ.

The Interpretation of Sacred Scripture

'St Jerome in his Study' - from a woodcut by Albrecht Dürer, 1492.

5

THE REVELATION OF GOD

When considering the Old Testament it is useful to think of the way in which the Ancient Israelites thought of their God through the ages. It is often assumed that the People of Israel had a complete and developed view of the nature of God from the very beginning. This would have been surprisingly novel and would go against our general belief that the truths of faith were gradually revealed to the people over time. If the world was to be prepared for the coming of Christ, an essential part of this would be the preparation of the people's faith.

The Ancient Near East was a world that believed in many gods. Most nations acknowledged a pantheon, which is a number of gods who lived in the celestial realm and interacted with each other. These gods also, to a greater or lesser extent, interacted with human beings.

One can understand this if one thinks of the development of human understanding of the world. If the world is confused and confusing then man's place within it mirrors that confused state. Why are there storm clouds which destroy the harvest and threaten the family? Why are there dangers from wild animals? Why are there diseases and suffering? What lives beyond the seas and in the heights of the mountains? All of these things were beyond the power of any individual mind and so they were invested with an unseen power which was ascribed to the realm of the gods.

We should not think that this is something which is external to the nature of man. He did not invent gods to understand the world. Rather the existence of gods, of supernatural forces, gave meaning to the world that he could see. Man has always believed in the existence of gods and has always conceived of himself in relationship with them.

Each unseen force, then, was divinised. In the Canaanite system of belief, sunrise and sunset were gods, as were the storm clouds. Fertility was the realm of a goddess (and to some extent the god, Ba'al), as was the fertility of the land. Each nation had its own gods and goddesses. And when one nation defeated another then the two pantheons could be combined or merged.

This seems to be the case with the ancestors of the Israelites. When Abraham left Ur of the Chaldeans to go to the Promised Land, he probably took with him household gods in the form of small idols. These are referred to in the arguments between Jacob and Laban about the stealing of the household gods (Genesis 31:19, 32, 35). It seems to have something to do with the proof of lineage. Elsewhere the use and possession of *teraphim* (the household gods) are specifically outlawed (II Kings 23:24).

We know that God had revealed Himself to Abraham, but at that time, there seems to have been no call for either an exclusive worship of God or a denial of the existence of other gods. Indeed if the revelation to Moses is anything to go by, it seems that Abraham and his two immediate descendants Isaac and Jacob may have worshipped three different gods, or the LORD under three different aspects.

The LORD, at the burning bush reveals himself to Moses as "I am the God of your father, the God of Abraham, the God of Isaac and the God of Jacob" (Exodus 3:6). Later He says that He appeared to Abraham and Isaac and Jacob under another name, God Almighty or *El Shaddai* (Exodus 6:3). Indeed different aspects of this revelation of God are given various names "the shield" of Abraham (Genesis 15:1) and "the Bull" or "Mighty One" of Jacob in Psalm 131.

The true revelation came only with the passage concerning the burning bush and Moses. Here the LORD reveals Himself as "the LORD". This is a new revelation of God, and will be considered in greater detail below.

The name of the LORD is interesting. First because it welds together the deity or deities of Abraham, Isaac and Jacob with the LORD Himself, but also because it gives a specific revelation to Moses which is new. And that new element is identified with a name.

In the Ancient Near East to have the name of something, and especially to know the name of a god gave a certain kind of power over it. Ba'al was the famous god of the Canaanites who was a challenge to the position of the LORD in the affections of the People of Israel. If, for example, you had a temple with a statue of the god Ba'al in it, and you wanted to invoke the god's help with storm clouds and the like then you could offer sacrifices, or as the prophets of Ba'al on Mount Carmel showed (I Kings 18:28), you could slash your flesh until the blood flowed. Much more effective, however, was calling on the name of the god. Then you had his attention. It is possible that this practice lay behind the prohibition in the Ten Commandments of "using the name of the LORD your God in vain" (Deuteronomy 5:11). Perhaps this was not originally a prohibition on blasphemy, but rather a ban on the use of the intimate name of the LORD with the intention of forcing Him into a certain action.

The revelation of the name of the LORD to Moses is a definite point in the religion of the Old Testament. Here at last is a God who can be identified and can be attached to His people.

The name of the LORD, as it is revealed, is obscure. It is not a personal name and does not seem to exist in any of the pantheons of the Ancient Near East. If the name is not personal, then neither, on the surface, is it terribly meaningful. In the revelation to Moses it runs something like; "I am that which I am", or because of the grammatical structure of Hebrew; "I cause to be that which I cause to be". In Hebrew this is אהיה אשר אהיה and when He refers to Himself in these passages, the LORD calls Himself "I am". In the rest of the Old Testament this is not the case. It changes from "I am" to "He is", and these four letters (יהוה) for which we do not have a correct pronunciation, is thenceforward the name of the LORD.

This name is called the Tetragrammaton, a grammatical and not a theological term, which means a four lettered word. As it is the name of God we call it the Divine Tetragrammaton. In the Revised Standard Version of the Bible it is rendered as the LORD in block capitals. Throughout this work, the Divine Tetragrammaton, the name that the LORD revealed to Moses will be referred to in that same way - the LORD.

The name was never really pronounced until recently in the last few centuries. First this occurred in theological circles. Then it found its way into Bibles (for example the Catholic Jerusalem Bible) and popular modern worship songs. For various reasons, not least the sensibilities of Jews, Ancient Christian practice and averting the danger of Marcionism, the practice of pronouncing of the name of the LORD has been recently forbidden by the Church in all public worship.

If the LORD was the God of the Israelites, this did not mean that there were not other gods, and to some extent, that these other gods did not have power and influence. We can see a remnant of this here:

> When the Most High gave to the nations their inheritance, when He separated the sons of men, He fixed the bounds of the peoples according to the number of the sons of God. For the LORD's portion is His people, Jacob His allotted heritage.
>
> Deuteronomy 32:8-9

Here, it seems that a god called the Most High (*El Elyon*) gave nations their deities to look after and protect them, and the deity which was given to Israel's son was the LORD. In later texts the LORD and *El Elyon* are identified as one and the same.

This passage is poetic in form and ancient in imagery. Other nations would have been given other protectors. We later see that this guardian of the People of Israel moves from being the LORD to being identified with the Archangel Michael in Daniel 12:1. It seems that other gods could exist, but the favoured one was the LORD.

From the belief that there may have been different gods ascribed to different nations, the next stage was to deny the power of the other gods, so that it was the LORD who was all powerful. Psalm 85 can show this stage of progression:

> There is none like Thee among the gods, O Lord,
> nor are there any works like Thine.
> All the nations Thou hast made shall come and bow down before Thee, O Lord, and shall glorify Thy name.
>
> Psalm 85:8

At this stage a belief in the reality of other gods may well exist, but they have no influence apart from the will of the LORD. It may be from this time that we have the strange exchange between the LORD and Satan in the beginning of the book of Job. Satan could have had no power himself, and so had to have been given the power to act by God. Satan was not a god, but he could function as a foil to God.

The final stage in the development of the LORD was the outright denial of the existence of other gods.

> I am the LORD, and there is no other, besides Me there is no God; I gird you, though you do not know Me.
>
> Isaiah 45:5

This is the true development of the revelation of the nature of God to His chosen people. At various times and in various stages God showed more of Himself and His nature to His people so that they could be brought to a fuller and more complete understanding of His purpose and identity. It would have been nonsense to have said to Abraham that not only was there one all powerful God but that the other gods, the gods of the nations, did not actually exist. It is only after theological revelation that the Israelites could fully grasp this.

First there was polytheism: a belief in many gods. This gave way to monolatry: there may be many gods but ours is best and should be worshipped to the exclusion of others. Finally monotheism was revealed as the true way of worshipping God.

That we see this later view of monotheism written into almost every page of the Old Testament is a testimony to the process of redaction (re-writing texts from a later point of view).

The name of God and the process of the revelation were so embedded in the cultural history of the Israelites that a whole-scale expunging simply could not take place.

What we know to be true later in life does not eradicate what we may have believed when we were not so developed. Truth, even of the nature of God, can only be accepted when the individual is capable of receiving it.

The Revelation of God

An image from a children's Colouring Book published in the nineteenth century. This is the moment when the LORD speaks to Moses through the burning bush and reveals His Name.

6

The Sources of the Old Testament

One of the most influential ways of looking at the Old Testament is commonly called the "Source/Documentary Hypothesis". It is most often ascribed to the work of the German theologian Julius Wellhausen.

This theory takes seriously the compilation of the Old Testament. It does not assume that any text, let alone book, of the Old Testament was given at any one time to any one person. The traditional assumption that Moses was the author of the first five books, the *Torah*, was seen to be theologically and historically flawed. The more the theologians looked at the texts, especially in the first five books, the more they saw that there were certain tendencies and patterns in the texts. Particular names for God were preferred one over the other, and even mountains were called different things in different narratives. For example, Mount Sinai is also called Mount Horeb.

It was not simply linguistic terms which brought about this view. There are duplicate stories, such as Sarah's relationships with foreign Kings (Genesis 12 and 20), not to mention the two creation accounts placed side by side in the beginning of the book of Genesis.

The Sources of the Old Testament

The hypothesis, for such it remains, may be outlined very broadly as follows.

Different strands of oral or written material came from different places and different times in the history of the People of God. These were recorded and developed in various ways and for various purposes. Four such sources may be identified.

The first is called "J". This source uses the Tetragrammaton for the name of the LORD. It takes its name from the German *Jahwist*. This is thought to be the oldest source. God is described in very human terms and the Hebrew is very poetic. The images that it uses are vivid and fresh. It is concerned with the Tribe/Kingdom of Judah. If one were to place a date on the source, it would be around 1000BC.

The second source is called "E". This source does not use the name of the LORD before the revelation to Moses at the burning bush, but rather refers to Him as "God" which in Hebrew is *El* or *Elohim*. It is dated a little later than "J" and is concerned with the Northern Kingdom and the priestly cult at Shiloh. Like "J" it is poetic in tone and imagery.

The third source is called "D" which stands for the Deuteronomists. They are often associated with finding the Temple scroll in the time of the restoration of the Temple by King Josiah in the middle of the seventh century BC. This Temple scroll, though not identified as such explicitly, is sometimes assumed to be the book of Deuteronomy. The source "D", however, is broader than one book. It is a group which is concerned with writing a religious history of the People of God.

The source is typified by concern with "law" and the keeping of the law as the outward sign that the People of God are faithful to the LORD. If the law is kept, the people will be rewarded by the promises of God. Their stylistic name for God is "The Lord Our God".

The Deuteronomists are not really to be identified with one particular group of people or scribes, who were working on one specific task at any one time. Rather it is probably better to think of these individuals as part of a trend within the scribal system to take the annals and historical data, either in written or oral form, and to record them reflecting the surrounding concerns. In any system, this would show the influence of the people who selected material in the way in which it was placed and written.

The final source in the documentary hypothesis is called "P" meaning the Priestly Source. This source seems to come from the specific period of the Babylonian exile (586-537BC). When the people were exiled they faced a period of self searching. Babylon contained not only the Jews, but also all of the leading citizens of the other nations that the Babylonians had conquered. In order to stop the process of assimilation, the Jewish priestly cast recorded the names of tribes and their descendants. The Priests' lists were not only historical in nature, but also performed a function of social identity. These genealogies were often combined with specific places. Identity is not just ancestry but also geography. The Patriarch Abraham fell into the period of pre-history. By identifying with him through blood and land, the Priests reinforced the historical identity of the people. It reminds the Jews of who they were and where they came from.

This "P" source is also responsible, within this theory, for collecting rites and rituals in minute detail. The book of Leviticus is often ascribed to "P". The depiction of God in these sections is distant. He is mediated through the action of priests, and especially priests of the line of Aaron. This emphasis on the transcendence of God is seen as a later development in Old Testament theology. It stands in contrast to the earlier depictions of God where He is described in almost human terms.

If "P" can be placed at this period then it serves to cement the identity of a community in exile. It looks back to their history in the Promised Land and also to a future restoration.

This is a very simple way of working with the sources of the Old Testament. If we agree that the texts of the Old Testament were not presented from on high, then some form of moulding or formation needs to have taken place. Any group of people will collect and preserve stories which are of interest to them. "J" seems to be concerned with the south and "E" with the north. These very early stories and histories would originally have been oral in nature. They needed at some point to be collated and recorded. Whoever did this put their own slant on the material that they gathered. As we have seen, the Deuteronomists emphasised the law, and the Priestly source emphasised the role of the priesthood.

Of course it is not as simple as this. Throughout the whole process of passing on texts, the texts themselves were constantly refined and changed.

Source theory allows this process to take place, and tries to see where, when and how these changes occur.

We must speak a word of caution here. We need to see the final text as the result of the process that was intended in the mind of God, while at the same time trying to find out how this final text came about. In this way one can attempt to see the intention of the people involved in the construction of the Old Testament and also the purpose of God in its preservation and development.

The Sources of the Old Testament

Engraving 'The Confusion of Tongues' by Gustave Doré (1865).

The Old Testament

7

History

With the rise of Biblicism, that is looking at the text of the Bible almost as a historical and scientific manual, the historical aspects of the Sacred Scriptures gain a great importance. Many of the other types of literature (especially the section that we will look at called 'Myth and Legend') are subsumed within it.

Here we will limit ourselves to those sections of the Old Testament which would describe themselves as history and those fragments of history found elsewhere.

The historical books are Joshua, Judges, Ruth, I and II Samuel, I and II Kings, I and II Chronicles, Ezra, Nehemiah, Esther and I and II Maccabees. In some older Catholic versions of the Bible some of these books are known by different names. The Book of the Kings, divided into four parts (I, II, III, IV Kings) in newer editions became I and II Samuel, and I and II Kings. I and II Chronicles were known as I and II Paralipomenon (the 'things left out'). We will use the modern terms for the names of the books of the Old Testament.

In looking at the way in which the Old Testament uses historical narrative we will provide an overview of the history of the people of Israel, from the call of Abraham to the time just before the birth of Our Saviour.

It is useful to go through the whole of the history of Israel to put names and places into some form of time scale. In doing this the time line that we will use will be quite conservative. We will use the texts of the Old Testament as the indicators of what happened and at roughly what time. Within Old Testament studies there are wild variations as to when historical actions took place, and indeed in some circles, whether or not they actually took place in the first place.

We will not begin this section of history with the creation of the world and what may be described as 'pre-history' for two reasons. First because even if this can be dated, it is an exceedingly long time until one gets any form of reliable documentation, either oral or written. Second because this section of the Old Testament will be dealt with later under the title Myth and Legend.

The Patriarchs

Our starting point is the call of Abraham, described in Genesis 12. As a date, we may guess at some time around the nineteenth to seventeenth centuries BC. Abraham is addressed by God as follows:

> Now the LORD said to Abram, "Go from your country and your kindred and your father's house to the land that I will show you. And I will make of you a great nation, and I will bless you, and make your name great, so that you will be a blessing. I will bless

those who bless you, and him who curses you I will curse; and by you all the families of the earth shall bless themselves."
So Abram went, as the LORD had told him…
Genesis 12:1-4a

There is no reason given by God for the choice of Abraham, and no real indication of who Abraham was. There is a genealogy of Abraham given before God's call, but all this does is place Abraham in relation to a list of names and puts him geographically in Ur of the Chaldeans. Ur is a city in modern day Iraq. Its people worshipped a pantheon of gods under the Sumerian belief system. This way of worshipping gods was common in the Ancient Near East. Around 2000BC Ur grew to be one of the largest cities in the known world because of trade. According to some estimates it numbered over 50,000 people. It may be that either dynastic struggles or lack of space was an external impetus to the migration of Abraham, as well as the internal call of God.

A note may be made here about these genealogies which one sees throughout the historical works of the Old Testament. Just because they are concerned with a time when there were no written records does not mean that they are inaccurate or incorrect. We know that ancient civilizations were capable of retaining vast amounts of oral information which would be quite impossible for us today. As with all Old Testament data, however, we have to treat it with a certain scepticism; it may or may not be accurate. The ages of the people listed is a separate issue. The longevity of the people mentioned seems to do with the amount of time that had passed since the age of pre-history. Many cultures describe their ancient ancestors living for an exceedingly long time. This will be discussed more fully below. The closer one gets to 'now', whenever now may be, the shorter their lives. Things were always better in the past!

So Abraham set out from his home under the promise of God to be the father of a great nation, and embarked on his journey. He ended up south of Jerusalem near Hebron. His life would have been one of nomadic sheep and cattle herding. This is not a settled existence, even though he bought a burial ground in Genesis 23 which may imply a certain stability. Abraham is important as he is the first of the Patriarchs. All of the tribes take their fundamental identity from him.

Abraham bore two sons. The first was by his slave girl Hagar. Sarah his wife was too old to bear children, and so Abraham had relations with Hagar so that his name would continue. The resulting son from this union between Abraham and Hagar was called Ishmael. At the age of thirteen Ishmael was circumcised and so was included in the promise of God through this external covenantal sign. Soon after, however, Sarah became pregnant with Isaac. According to some versions of the law, Ishmael had a right of inheritance, but as he was not a son by Abraham and Sarah, Sarah was concerned for the position of her own child. Accordingly, after much wrangling, Sarah's will prevailed and Hagar and Ishmael were sent forth into the wilderness of Paran, where they were looked after by an angel of God (Genesis 21).

The Old Testament

The stage was now clear for the second son, Isaac, to take his position as inheritor of the promise to Abraham. Abraham's love and obedience to the LORD was tested when he was asked to take the boy to the land of Moriah and sacrifice him. This action has great significance as a type, or foreshadowing, of the sacrifice of Christ. This will be looked at a little later in the section 'Apocalypse and the coming of Christ'.

To continue through the generations, Isaac's wife, Rebecca, gave birth to twins, Esau and Jacob. Although Esau was the firstborn, the blessing fell on Jacob, after a spot of trickery and dressing in animal skins. We notice, of course, that this is the second time that the blessing comes through the second son and not the first. This may be a way for later generations to try to understand why and how they found themselves the People of God, when strict genealogy would place the blessing on others.

Jacob's name was changed to Israel. The change came about after a strange wrestling match between Jacob and an angel of the LORD.

It is Jacob/Israel who has the sons who are to become the foundation pillars of the twelve tribes of Israel. They are: Reuben, Simeon, Levi, Judah, Dan, Naphtali, Gad, Asher, Issachar, Zebulun, Joseph and Benjamin. He also had a daughter called Dinah. The deeds of these individuals, with the exception of Joseph, are not terribly important. Much more so is the clear association of later Jewish identity with the sons of Israel. All of the People of God could trace their identities to these twelve men and the land was divided up among these tribes.

Here one runs into one of the problems occasionally found in the Old Testament. Everyone throughout history knows that there are twelve tribes. Much of the later Old Testament identity of the People of God is founded upon this. However, there were at least two other tribes who had allotments of land. They were Ephraim and Manasseh. These were the sons of Joseph. They are mentioned in the lists of the tribes. The first chapter of the book of Numbers lists a census that is to be taken by Moses. The sons of Joseph are mentioned individually but the number of tribes is not thirteen, as it should be. One tribe has been excluded; the Tribe of Levi. The reason for this is given thus,

> To the tribe of Levi alone Moses gave no inheritance;
> the offerings by fire to the LORD God of Israel are
> their inheritance, as He said to him.
>
> Joshua 13:14

The sons of Levi are removed from the tribes who are to receive an inheritance because their role is one of priesthood. It is they who are to minister to the sanctuary of God, first in the wilderness and later in the Temple. There may be a number of reasons for this. Some have suggested that Levi was not originally a tribe at all and was only added in later. This seems highly unlikely as the names of the Twelve Tribes are so fixed in the Old Testament psyche. More likely is a plain reading of the Old Testament. All of the tribes should have had a geographical portion of the land. However this had never been allotted to the tribe of Levi. Later to fill this gap and make sure that there were twelve sections in the land, the half tribe of Manasseh was included.

Moses

The history of Israel continued as the tribes decamped into Egypt because of famine in the Promised Land. This was not uncommon in the Ancient Near East where the harvest was unstable. We can guess at a date sometime before the sixteenth century BC. It should not come as a great surprise that these nomadic people moved freely across borders which themselves were not clearly fixed. We have to ask the question, which has implications for a later period in the history of Israel, whether or not all of the People of God moved to Israel. The Bible seems to imply that, if not all, then a significant number of people went from the land of Canaan and settled in the land of Egypt.

It seems unlikely that this predominantly nomadic people, with strong family ties, but loose organisational structures, would move *en masse*. It is more than possible that some, but not all, of the People of Israel went down to Egypt. When the Old Testament was recorded some time later it would be assumed that the great deeds which the LORD brought about to save his people would have involved everyone. These were the real foundational actions of God in relation to the People.

The stage is set for the arrival of Moses. He was not one of the Patriarchs, but was the real spiritual head and leader of the People of God. His role cannot be over-emphasised.

Who then was Moses?

Moses' father had been a Levite and we know that Moses had a brother named Aaron, and a sister called Miriam. His father having died, Moses' mother Jochebed tried to hide him from a purge of Hebrew boys. The killing was undertaken on the orders of Pharaoh. His mother placed him in a basket made of bulrushes and he was entrusted to the river. He was rescued by Pharaoh's daughter and grew up in her household. One day, seeing a Hebrew being cruelly treated by an Egyptian overlord, Moses killed the Egyptian and fled into the wilderness (Exodus 2). Here he sheltered with distant relations and married a Midianite woman called Zipporah.

What follows is the decisive event in the foundation stories of the People of God. The LORD revealed Himself to Moses in the midst of the burning bush. Something of the importance of this name has been mentioned above. More than this, however, the LORD gave Moses the task of rescuing His people from Egypt and leading them into the Promised Land. This he had to do by a series of threats and by cajoling Pharaoh, which ended in the great plagues of Egypt. It would be very important that this 'new' God proved Himself. Even though the LORD had identified Himself with the God of Abraham, Isaac and Jacob, His power was still unverified. It is through the foundational acts that He showed Himself to be a God who was worthy of being followed and who had shown Himself to be committed to the People of Israel.

What is the historicity of these events? Bluntly we do not know. We do not need to try to 'prove' that they happened or did not. They are the deeds of God in His governance of the universe to bring the People of God from the land of Egypt to the Promised Land.

We have extra-Biblical texts that refer to the 'Habiru' understood variously as a slave tribe who rebelled against Pharaoh, or as mercenaries who attacked Egypt. It was fashionable for a time, when these texts were first discovered, to assume that this must have been a reference to the Hebrews. This is now thought unlikely as the term seem to be more generic rather than descriptive of a specific people. Iconographically they are shown as a horse riding people, skilled in the use of the bow. This does not seem to be in harmony with what we know of the People of God.

The defining action of this new God occurs at this time: the Crossing of the Red Sea. This is constantly referred to throughout the Old Testament. Theories abound as to what this means. Is it the Red Sea, or the Sea of Reeds? Was there a miracle with water to the left and right of the Israelites, or was it simply that the wheels of Pharaoh's chariots got stuck in the mud, followed by an inundation of water which led to a minor drowning, just enough for Pharaoh's army to turn back? Many of these speculations arise from the attempt to prove that the Old Testament is historically accurate. However, we know this is not the purpose of Old Testament historical narrative. It does not matter how exactly it happened, the important thing is that God intervened and saved His people. It was this decisive fact which was worth recording.

What we know for certain is that few if any of the historical works in the Old Testament which deal with historical accounts actually date from the time of the action which they describe. Indeed one is much more likely to find historical truth in poetry and song relating to historical events than in the history books. Let us consider the passage concerning the crossing of the Red Sea:

> Then Moses and the people of Israel sang this song to the LORD, saying, "I will sing to the LORD, for He has triumphed gloriously; the horse and his rider He has thrown into the sea. The LORD is my strength and my song, and He has become my salvation; this is my God, and I will praise Him, my father's God, and I will exalt Him. The LORD is a man of war; the LORD is His name. "Pharaoh's chariots and his host He cast into the sea; and his picked officers are sunk in the Red Sea. The floods cover them; they went down into the depths like a stone. Thy right hand, O LORD, glorious in power, Thy right hand, O LORD, shatters the enemy.
>
> Exodus 15:1-6

We know that this song within the historical narrative is older than the section which surrounds it. Songs remain in society's consciousness much longer than other things. One of the best ways to remember events is in song. That this section is specifically mentioned as a song is important.

Further, it can give validity to the history which does surround it. People would be able to say, 'Yes that is the song that we sing about Pharaoh and the Red Sea'. This gives greater weight to the historical events, the detail. If you think of the process in the opposite direction then it is a little more problematic. If the historian or storyteller suddenly declares that this song was sung when the Israelites stood on dry land and the forces of Pharaoh were shattered, and his audience has never heard it before, then he would not be believed. Why invent a song which does not need to be there? The Israelites do not break into song when they enter the Promised Land, or when the walls of Jericho fall down. So why should they here? Unless of course there is a pre-existing song about this event, which can be woven into a historical narrative.

If this is the case then there are historical facts that can be gathered from it. Even if the song does not date from the time of the Crossing of the Red Sea, its historical nature shows that whenever it was composed certain elements were included. The sea was involved as were horses and chariots. At no time is the drowning of Pharaoh mentioned.

If this is what we can glean from the song, then its point is to stress the power of the LORD and the salvation of the people. We know that the whole of the song, even though it may be older than other sections, is not from the time that it claims because it ends with the following passage "Thou wilt bring them in and plant them on Thy holy mountain, the place, O LORD, which Thou Hast made for Thy abode, the Sanctuary O LORD which Thy hands have established." v.17. As this clearly refers to the capture of Jerusalem some four or five centuries later by King David and the building of the Temple by his son King Solomon, it cannot be an original section of the song sung by the Israelites who had just been saved from Pharaoh's chariots and horsemen.

Another aspect of this song which would incline us to think that it is an early fragment, is the manner in which the LORD is described. He is seen very much in human terms. He is a warrior, a strong man. This rather simple view of God became much more refined as the history of Israel progressed. We shall look at this in the section on 'Myth and Legend'.

Standing back from this particular piece of historical writing, we can see that there is a problem with sections of the Old Testament which deal with the older times. If there are problems when looking at something as relatively recent as the flight from Egypt, how many more problems will arise when looking at the times of the Patriarchs, Abraham, Isaac and Jacob? How are we to understand, for example the destruction of Sodom and Gomorrah? Or the genealogies which ascribe the heritage of certain tribes?

One temptation which must be resisted is simply to throw up one's hands in horror and say that as we cannot know anything for certain, then we cannot know anything at all, and to dismiss huge sections of the Old Testament as historically unreliable.

This would be unfair to those sections of history. We know that although they may well have been recorded in written form centuries and centuries after the events they describe, nonetheless the ability to remember collectively is something for which the peoples of the Old Testament and more ancient civilizations generally are well known. We in our day have problems remembering one or two generations back. One only has to go to a family gathering to remember stories and events which have lain long hidden in our minds. As our lives became more isolated and we become surrounded by people who are not of our family, clan and tribe, so the connections that bind us together become forgotten. We rely on written forms of history rather than oral forms, and once lost, oral forms are exceedingly difficult to re-learn. They can be placed into the realm where we scarcely believe they are possible. We begin to scoff at the suggestion that historical facts or genealogies or events can be accurately remembered over many hundreds of years. This is a modern problem and should not be read back into the abilities or otherwise of the peoples of the Old Testament.

Although we can see inconsistencies in historical accounts, this is no reason to dismiss them out of hand. Looking positively, it should help guard against accepting historical Biblical truth as if it came from one of our modern text books.

We can accept that when later generations came to transcribe their oral history they found some things which puzzled them. To try to understand these elements, they may have interposed other literature or traditions to explain something which did not fit in with their world view.

The purpose of the Moses narratives is so much greater than mere historical fact, or the writing of a mere history book. These are the fundamental foundation stories of the people. The great saving act of being brought through the Red Sea formed the people. It was preceded by the revelation of the very name of

God, a name, remember, which became so holy that no-one could even pronounce it. The significance of the revelation of the name cannot be underestimated. This was the precondition of the sealing of the covenant between the LORD and His people in the ceremony at Mount Sinai. Moses himself had ratified the covenant by throwing blood on the people (Exodus 24).

It was in the wilderness that the Ten Commandments were given to the people and all of the later cultic objects came to be forged: the Ark of the Covenant, the Tent of Meeting, the cultic pole *nehushtan* topped by the bronze serpent, Aaron's flowering rod and others not mentioned.

But the wilderness was only a means to an end. Moses' primary role was to bring about the fulfilment of the Abrahamic covenant; which promised that Abraham's descendants would be as numberless as the stars. At this point in history, more than before, this covenant became connected with the land. Not only will the descendants be great, but also they will dwell in the land, the Promised Land. This is a development of the original promise of God to Abraham. Originally it had been that Abraham would have descendants, only later did it become connected with the land.

It is a historical oddity that it is not Moses who leads the people into the Promised Land but someone else. Moses died on Mount Nebo in Moab looking down onto the land, into which Joshua, son of Nun was to lead the people. This seems to be one plain historical fact that everyone remembers. It was not Moses, but Joshua who led the entry. Theologically it should have been

Moses as this was the role that seemed to have been assigned to him. Historically it was not. So instead of just saying that Moses died in the wilderness and Joshua took his place, a story is found in an attempt to give a theological explanation to a historical act.

The story is related in Numbers 20. When the people were thirsty in the desert they asked Moses why he had brought them into this land if they were just to die of thirst. Moses went to the Tent of Meeting and the LORD told him to go and strike the rock. Moses did so and water flowed forth. The Lord then said to Moses:

> Because you did not believe in Me, to sanctify Me in the eyes of the people of Israel, therefore you shall not bring this assembly into the land which I have given them.
>
> Numbers 20:12

The issue seems to be that Moses did not have enough faith to realise that God would eventually provide water and would not let the people die of thirst. It was his lack of faith that brought about this action of the LORD. The Israelites had complained to the LORD before, of course. In the first case when manna rained from heaven (Exodus 16) it was the LORD who had provided food without being prompted. When they had grown tired of manna (Numbers 21:4ff), Moses had interceded for the people before the LORD to assuage His anger. This was important for the internal logic of the story. It was on behalf of the people and not through a lack of faith that Moses intervened. It was taken for granted that the LORD would ultimately take care of the people that He had brought up out of the land of Egypt.

This anger of the LORD seems to be a disproportionate overreaction, and so may be a way of trying to explain why Joshua and not Moses led the People of God into the Promised Land that was understandable to later generations.

The Tribes in the Promised Land and the Rise of Kingship

The People of God entered the land with mighty wars and great victories, according to the Biblical narrative. Here we may remember a comment made above concerning whether or not all of the descendants of Abraham went down into the land of Egypt. If they did, then all of the People of God entered into the land at this moment. If some had stayed in Canaan and not gone down into Egypt, then only one section was now entering the land from the wilderness. They could have called on family ties with those who had stayed in Canaan. This would explain a little better how this army of the People of God could crush all the peoples described in the Old Testament.

As the People of God were still primarily tribal units when the land was apportioned, it was split along tribal lines. Joshua 15*ff* goes into great detail on this subject. Note that there seems to be thirteen sections on the map of the tribal Allotments. There were no sections for Levi or Joseph. The Tribe of Levi was excluded because their portion was to serve the LORD as priests, and Joseph did not have a single inheritance, as it was divided between his sons, Ephraim and Manasseh. There was a double section for the tribe of Manasseh even though they were described as a half tribe.

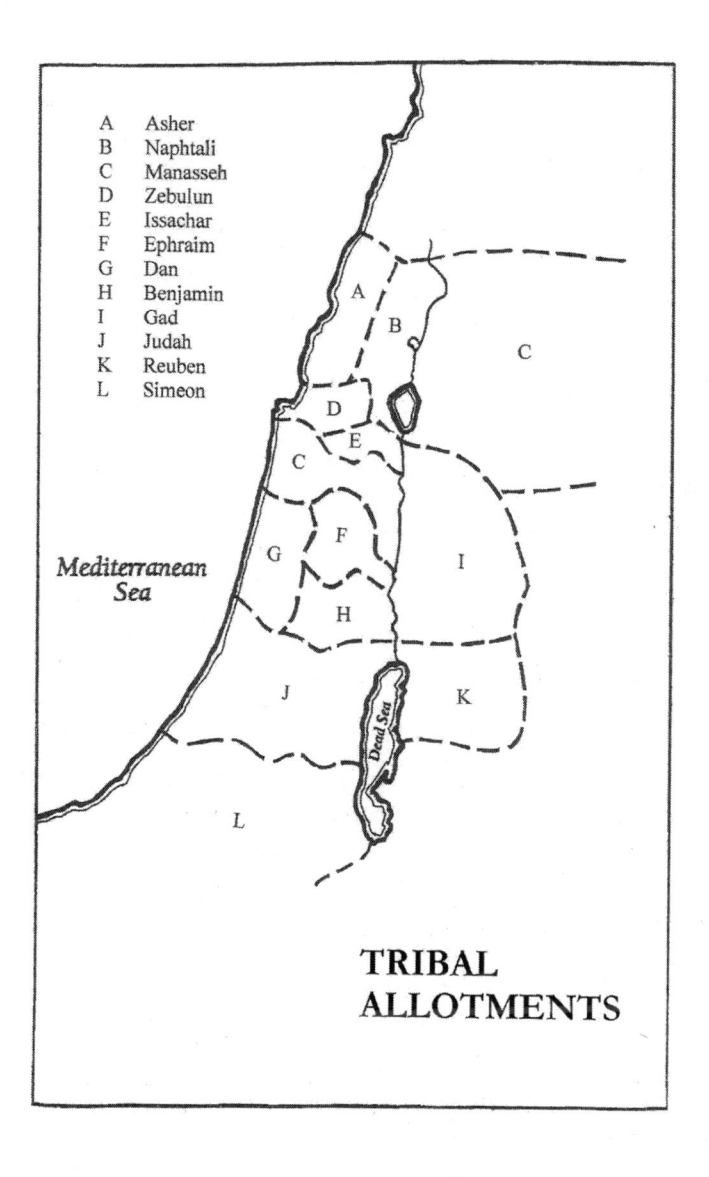

A	Asher
B	Naphtali
C	Manasseh
D	Zebulun
E	Issachar
F	Ephraim
G	Dan
H	Benjamin
I	Gad
J	Judah
K	Reuben
L	Simeon

TRIBAL ALLOTMENTS

These tribal divisions served the people quite well from the twelfth century BC onwards. The tribes lived a semi autonomous lifestyle in relation to one other. When, as the People of God, they were attacked they could come together and defend their own territory and that of their tribal brothers. The overall structure was predominantly defensive. Each had their own holy places and inner tribal structure.

The ancient Israelites were distinguished from the lands around them by not having a unified nation. They did not have a King. This tribal nature of the People of God was something clearly prized. The importance of tribes is seen in the constant reference to tribal history when describing any individual character. They came together for festival or war, but were not unified by any other ties, either economic or political.

While a loose confederation of tribes was fine for certain political circumstances, it was not the most robust entity. The tribes moved from this structure to one of monarchy, a model which was found in the nations that surround them. It may well have been that it was not jealousy of the other nations that brought them to desire a King, but rather expediency.

This desire however was against the express wish of the LORD. It was the LORD who was the King of Israel, not a man. Antecedent to the monarchy a certain unity had already been seen. There had been a united leadership under Samuel in response to the Philistine threat. As so often happens when a charismatic leader dies, Samuel's replacement had to be similarly charismatic. The era of the Judges ensued. The leadership of the Judges after

The Old Testament

Samuel gives us famous names such as Gideon, Jephthah and Samson. In I Samuel we have the addition of two other Judges, Eli, the priest of Shiloh, and Samuel himself. If we wish to date this extended era of the Judges, it can conservatively be placed between 1200 to 1000 BC.

> The people refused to listen to the voice of Samuel; and they said, " No! but we will have a King over us, that we also may be like all the nations, and that our King may govern us and go out before us and fight our battles."
> And when Samuel had heard all the words of the people, he repeated them in the ears of the LORD. And the LORD said to Samuel, "Hearken to their voice, and make them a King." Samuel then said to the men of Israel, "Go every man to his city."
> I Samuel 8:19-22

A King is suitably chosen, Saul by name. Although there is a certain amount of material concerning Saul in the historical texts, it seems more like a prelude than a paean of praise. As Saul fell into what seems to us to be a kind of mental disorder and disease, the stage was set for the coming of King David.

King David

King David burst onto the field ruddy of cheek and fair of face (I Samuel 16) and his deeds from the very outset were the thing of legend. It was he who killed Goliath and saved the nation. It was he who was lauded by the people. He was the only one who could soothe King Saul by playing on stringed instruments. To all intents and purposes, it was David who was the first real King of Israel worthy of the title. Nevertheless, King Saul could not just be written out of the history and made to disappear.

The great King David took Jerusalem by force and set it up as his capital and administrative centre. In doing this David showed a political astuteness. This was a new capital for a new King, and more importantly, a united capital for a united Kingdom. David's prowess was in war, and through conquest he managed not only to expand, but also to secure, the borders of the nation. This was a new political reality. Together the tribes could do more than they could achieve individually. With military successes came political consequences. To defend their newly won lands, the tribes had to pay allegiance to the centre, to King David.

King David also secured his role by associating Jerusalem not only with his own royal person, but also with God. Throughout the long sojourn in the wilderness the LORD had been with His people in a very tangible way. He had used various objects to manifest His power: the Ark, the Tablets, The Flowering Rod and *nehushtan*.

These objects were in the safe keeping of the different tribes. They were the centre around which the Tribes' individual worship revolved. King David's genius was to bring all of these objects together into one place. That place was bound up with the new political regime, namely Jerusalem.

In this context we can read the account of the prophecy of Nathan:

> Now when the King dwelt in his house, and the LORD had given him rest from all his enemies round about, the King said to Nathan the prophet, "See now, I dwell in a house of cedar, but the ark of God dwells in a tent."
> But that same night the word of the LORD came to Nathan, "Go and tell My servant David, 'Thus says the LORD: Would you build Me a house to dwell in? I have not dwelt in a house since the day I brought up the people of Israel from Egypt to this day, but I have been moving about in a tent for My dwelling.' Now therefore thus you shall say to My servant David, 'Thus says the LORD of hosts, I took you from the pasture, from following the sheep, that you should be prince over My people Israel; and I have been with you wherever you went, and have cut off all your enemies from before you; and I will make for you a great name, like the name of the great ones of the earth. When your days are fulfilled and you lie down with your fathers, I will raise up your offspring after you, who shall come forth from your body, and I will establish his Kingdom. He shall build a house for My name, and I will establish the throne of his Kingdom for ever. I will be his father, and he shall be My son. When he commits iniquity, I will chasten him with the rod of men, with the stripes of the sons of men; but I will not take My steadfast love from him, as I took it from Saul, whom I put away from before you. And your house and your Kingdom shall be made sure for ever before Me; your throne shall be established for ever."
>
> II Samuel 7:1-16

On the surface this is quite clear. King David's fame would not come from building the Temple, but rather from having a dynasty after him. If this is historically accurate then all is well and good, but we have other accounts of why David did not build the Temple. In I Kings 5 King Solomon summons Hiram, King of

Tyre, to ask for skilled labourers to work on the building project. He gives a reason why this temple had not been built previously. "You know that David my father could not build a house for the name of the LORD his God because of the warfare with which his enemies surrounded him..."

This may seem a small point but it shows that when the historians came to write down an account of the time of King David, they could not give a good enough reason why he had not built the Temple. He had the money and resources and he had the political influence. King Solomon's speech gives one answer. He was simply too busy fighting with the nations surrounding him, and the building of a Temple was low on his priorities. He already had all of the religious objects and the allegiance of the tribes which the objects signified. King David was simply getting on with what King David did best: fighting.

When the historians tried to give an account of this period there was an explanation of sorts, but not a satisfactory one. Some centuries later, the Temple had taken on a mythic status. This was the place where God dwelt. This was the "true pole of the earth". Nothing greater or more significant existed in the whole of the world, and it was symbolised by the presence of the Ark of the Covenant. How could the greatest King of all, whose descendants would be the LORD's own anointed, have neglected the greatest symbol of the presence of God? In the words reportedly spoken by King David to Nathan the prophet "I dwell in a house of cedar, while the Ark of God dwells in a tent." How could their great and mighty King have allowed this to happen?

The answer was simple. There must have been a prophecy, and that prophecy must have explained why the LORD did not want King David to build the Temple. For good measure it would also give King David a promise, a covenant for his successive generations. This prophecy provides an adequate explanation.

History can readily be made to reflect a later reality which was not necessarily present at the time, but which 'must have been true'.

We can see the way that generations changed texts because of later theological truth throughout the Old Testament. One example is changing the name of one of Saul's sons. In one version of history, he is called 'Ish-bosheth', for example in II Samuel 2:10, and in another he is called 'Ash-ba'al' or 'Esh-ba'al' in I Chronicles 8:33. Why do these two accounts have different names for the same person? The answer seems to be in the second half of his name. The first part 'Ish', 'Ash' or 'Esh' can all mean more or less the same thing, 'man of'. 'Bosheth' or 'Ba'al' is much more interesting. The first means something like 'shame', the second is the name of the Canaanite god who caused the Israelites so many problems. All through the pages of the Old Testament there is a constant call on the people to stop worshipping the foreign gods of the nations and to turn again to the LORD their God. The people seemed to have an excessive fondness for the god Ba'al and his consort Asherah/Athirat, the goddess of fertility. It seems then, that Saul's son was actually called Ash-ba'al but this was subsequently changed to Ish-bosheth. The later redactors (editors) would have changed the *ba'al* suffix to *bosheth*; that Saul's son bore the name of a foreign god had brought 'shame' (*bosheth*) on the nation.

To return to King David, his importance was not so much strengthening the borders of the nation which took place under his Kingship, but the symbol which he represented. Even though the end of David's reign was not glorious, what survived him was not the Kingdom but the promises that were attached to it, specifically the promises attached to his line. This is the beginning of the Davidic covenant and Messianic promises. These will be looked at below in the section on the Apocalypse and the Coming of Christ.

The land which King David left behind was stable. It was moderately successful economically, secure in its borders, firmly united under the monarchy after the shaky start of King Saul, and centred in the new capital Jerusalem.

King Solomon

In any period of history the transition from one ruler or King to another is a point of tension and potential disintegration. With Bathsheba and the influential court prophet Nathan on his side, and after a rather ruthless series of palace coups, the road was cleared for Solomon to become the new King of Israel. The transition seems to have been smooth if somewhat bloody. His claims to the throne were backed up by historical references such as the deathbed charge found below:

> I [David] am about to go the way of all the earth. Be strong, and show yourself a man, and keep the charge of the LORD your God, walking in His ways and keeping His statutes, His commandments, His ordinances, and His testimonies, as it is written in the law of Moses, that you may prosper in all that you do and wherever you turn; that the LORD may establish His word which He spoke concerning me, saying, 'If your sons take heed to their way, to walk before Me in faithfulness with all their heart and with all their soul, there shall not fail you a man on the throne of Israel.'
>
> I Kings 2:2-4

After a dynastic struggle, how convenient to discover such a speech! It certainly bolstered the legitimacy of this inheritance claim and can thus be treated with suitable caution.

Solomon was a very influential figure in the history of Israel. In many ways he was more important than King David. King David had secured the borders by war but it was King Solomon who stabilised the Kingdom that David had won. Solomon was known as a wise man This can be seen most graphically in his advice to cut a baby in half to determine the identity of the mother (I Kings 3). The result was that much of the Wisdom literature was ascribed to King Solomon: the Books of Proverbs, Ecclesiastes and the Song of Songs, as well as many Psalms.

Part of Solomon's political strategy was to ally himself by marriage with the foreign nations who could threaten him. Perhaps this is the source of his seven hundred wives and three hundred concubines (I Kings 11:3). One of his wives, of great political interest, was the daughter of the Pharaoh. Not only did this put him on good terms with one of the most powerful Kingdoms within striking distance, but it also opened up potential trade routes. King Solomon not only used marriage as a political tool, he also used trade. There was a trade in horses and chariots from Egypt in the south to the Hittite Kingdoms in the north. As Solomon's Kingdom was the corridor through which trade had to pass, he gained a monopoly over the provision of goods. The descriptions of the wealth of King Solomon may have been exaggerated somewhat but wealth did flood into the nation because of trade.

King Solomon's reputation for wisdom also came about because of the infrastructure which he developed in the Kingdom. This may well have come from Egypt, perhaps under the influence of Pharaoh's daughter. In a Kingdom so dependent upon trade, it was necessary for a literate civil service to grow and develop.

This nascent bureaucracy was based around the greatest feat in King Solomon's reign, namely the building of the Temple in Jerusalem. The theological significance of the Temple is extraordinary. As well as being a religious focus, it also concentrated the resources needed to record and administer a growing state, and provided a centralised treasury.

Finally Solomon is remembered for being the last King of the United Monarchy. After him the land split under his sons, Rehoboam and Jeroboam. In the South was the Kingdom of Judah (including the capital Jerusalem) under Rehoboam. In the North was the Kingdom of Israel, with its capital at Shechem, under the rule of Jeroboam. The sons had torn apart the Kingdom of their father and grandfather.

However, the spilt did not occur immediately.

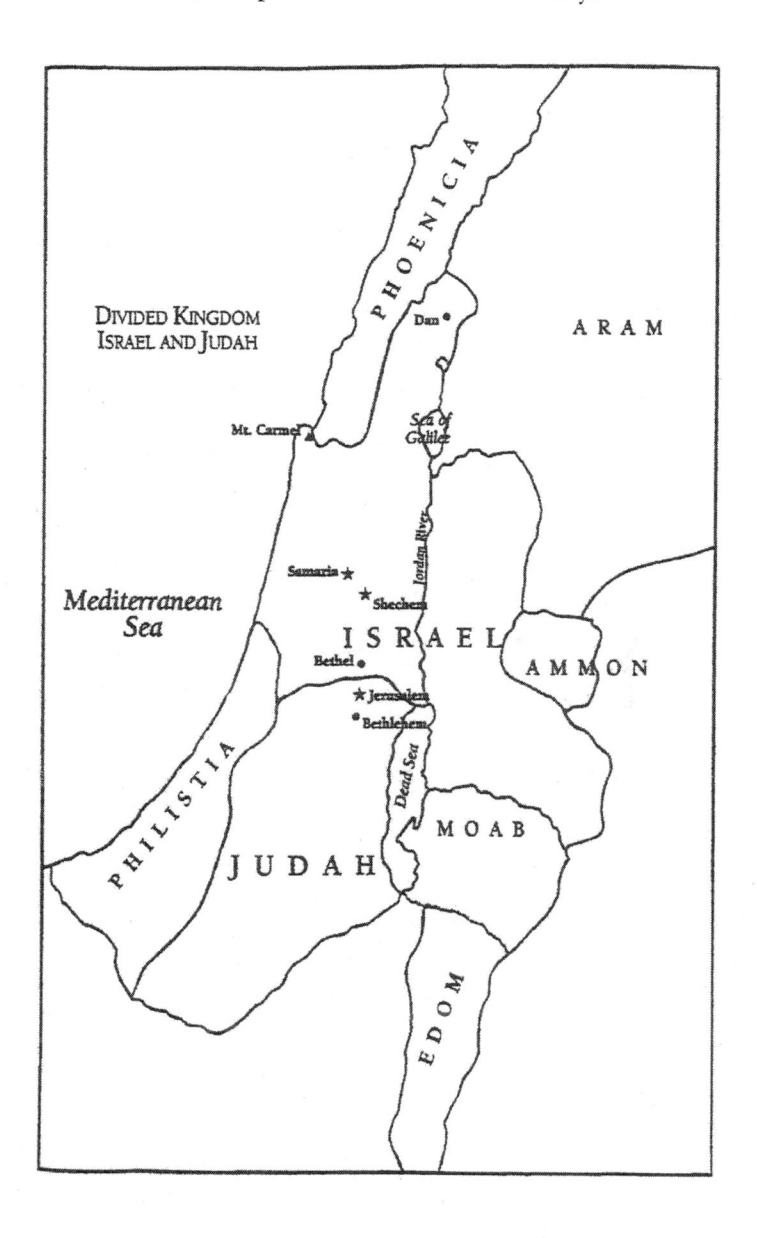

The Division of the Kingdom

There had been a cloak and dagger plot by the ten Northern Tribes (the Southern ones being Judah and Benjamin) during the latter years of King Solomon's reign. A suitable prophecy had been provided by Ahijah, accompanied by a symbolic tearing of garments and a theological justification. King Solomon, it seems, had been led astray by his many wives and concubines from the true worship of the LORD to the terrible practices of the Canaanites:

> Because he [Solomon] has forsaken Me, and worshipped Ashtoreth the goddess of the Sidonians, Chemosh the god of Moab, and Milcom the god of the Ammonites, and has not walked in My ways, doing what is right in My sight and keeping My statutes and My ordinances, as David his father did.
>
> I Kings 11:33

It seems likely that even at this time, there was a fair amount of syncretism (mixing of worship) in the land. Towards the end of his life King Solomon was said to go to the High Places and offer raisin cakes to the Queen of Heaven. These were religious practices of the people of Canaan and had nothing to do with the worship of the LORD. Solomon was to be suitably punished.

Historically such descriptions may reflect the religious practices in the country, seen from a later perspective. Strict monotheistic worship to the exclusion of all other deities was not enforced at this point in history. Looking back, any syncretism would have been considered unacceptable, so it is used as a way of explaining why terrible things happened at certain times. Why did the Kingdom split in half? It must have been the fault of King Solomon and those wicked raisin cakes.

Palace intrigues had been rumbling even in King Solomon's time. Jeroboam fled into exile to Egypt and when King Solomon died, the crown passed to his eldest son Rehoboam. One must remember that the Northern plot had involved Jeroboam, as a figure head who was now exiled. The gathering of the tribes for the investiture of the new King was fixed to take place in Shechem. Shechem had been the place of the covenant ceremony between the twelve tribes, but it was not connected with monarchy neither was it a temple site, such as Shiloh or indeed Jerusalem itself.

The choice of place seems to have been more political than religious. The strong Northern Tribes summoned Rehoboam from his stronghold in the South to their territory in the north. They demanded a relief from the taxation which Rehoboam had imposed immediately on his father's death. Rehoboam had to go to Shechem to be crowned, and while he was there, vulnerable in their territory, they addressed the issue of taxation. At the same time, knowing that rebellion was afoot, Jeroboam returned from exile in Egypt and pleaded the Northern Tribes' cause. Rehoboam's older advisors suggested relaxing the taxation regime, the younger firebrands told him to stick to his policy. The latter course was taken and fighting ensued. Rehoboam's commander Adoram was killed and Rehoboam fled to his capital in Jerusalem.

The Northern Tribes refused to acknowledge Rehoboam as King, and crowned Jeroboam in his stead.

The Kingdom was divided. In the South was the Kingdom of Judah, consisting of the Tribes of Judah and Benjamin, ruled over by King Rehoboam, and in the North was the Kingdom of Israel, consisting of the remaining Tribes, ruled over by King Jeroboam. The Northern Kingdom's capital was in Shechem, and their national shrines were in Bethel and Dan.

The Kingdom of Israel

Let us pursue the history of the Northern Kingdom of Israel until its destruction in 721BC.

The capital moved from place to place, first at Shechem, then to Tirza, then finally under King Omri, to Samaria. The Kings are listed quite sparsely in the Old Testament, together with the refrain that they did "what was evil in the sight of the LORD". Their various wickednesses are recorded, usually revolving around ignoring the worship of the LORD and following the gods of the Canaanites, notably the ever-popular Ba'al and Asherah. This reached a culmination under King Ahab when Elijah slew the prophets of Ba'al on Mount Carmel. Most of the sections of history in this period deal with the prophets Elijah and Elisha.

Finally in the year 721BC the Northern Kingdom came to an end. King Hoshea entered into vassalage with King Shalmaneser the Assyrian, but this did not continue, as Hoshea tried to double-cross his oppressors:

> But the King of Assyria found treachery in Hoshea; for he had sent messengers to So, King of Egypt, and offered no tribute to the King of Assyria, as he had done year by year; therefore the King of Assyria shut him up, and bound him in prison. Then the King of Assyria invaded all the land and came to Samaria, and for three years he besieged it. In the ninth year of Hoshea the King of Assyria captured Samaria, and he carried the Israelites away to Assyria, and placed them in Halah, and on the Habor, the river of Gozan, and in the cities of the Medes.
>
> II Kings 17:4-6

The Assyrian King, Sargon II, took the capital Samaria and with it the Northern Kingdom. He records "Samaria I looked at, I captured; 27,280 men who dwelt in it I carried away into Assyria." (from the Royal Annals of Assyria).

The Old Testament was more concerned in its history with the reason for the fall of the Northern Kingdom of Israel than any of the particular details and so the author of II Kings continued:

> And this was so, because the people of Israel had sinned against the LORD their God, who had brought them up out of the land of Egypt from under the hand of Pharaoh King of Egypt, and had feared other gods and walked in the customs of the nations whom the LORD drove out before the people of Israel, and in the customs which the Kings of Israel had introduced. And the people of Israel did secretly against the LORD their God things that were not right. They built for themselves high places at all their towns, from watchtower to fortified city; they set up for themselves pillars and Asherim on every high hill and under every green tree; and there they

> burned incense on all the high places, as the nations did whom the LORD carried away before them. And they did wicked things, provoking the LORD to anger, and they served idols, of which the LORD had said to them, "You shall not do this."
>
> II Kings 17:7-12

The Northern Kingdom had fallen to the Assyrians because they had not practised the worship of the LORD.

The people were dispersed throughout the empire, and their identity was lost.

The Kingdom of Judah

Let us turn to the Southern Kingdom under the leadership of Solomon's son Rehoboam. We left this Kingdom after the rebellion of the Northern Tribes. Although there were small-scale battles between the two Kingdoms, there was no out and out conflict. This may well have been because within five years Rehoboam's Kingdom of Judah was under attack by a much more dangerous invader:

> In the fifth year of King Rehoboam, Shishak King of Egypt came up against Jerusalem; he took away the treasures of the house of the LORD and the treasures of the King's house; he took away everything. He also took away all the shields of gold which Solomon had made; and King Rehoboam made in their stead shields of bronze...
>
> I Kings 14:25-27

This wholesale sacking of not only Jerusalem but the whole of the Kingdom of Judah was the defining moment in Rehoboam's reign. It should not be forgotten that his brother Jeroboam had found shelter in Egypt before returning and leading the Northern Tribes in the foundation of the Kingdom of Israel. How very convenient that in this moment of weakness, Jeroboam's enemy Rehoboam was attacked by his former protector.

The length of the reign of the Kings, according to the inner logic of the Old Testament, should reflect their fidelity to the worship of the LORD. The history should be simple. If a King does what is good in the eyes of the LORD, then he should live for a long time and rule with justice and right. Unfortunately this is not the case. Josiah, one of the best pre-exilic Kings in the eyes of those who reworked the Scriptures did not rule for anywhere near as long as King Manasseh, who was a thoroughly bad thing. Josiah reigned for thirty one years, a truly prodigious amount of time in the Old Testament period but King Manasseh seems to have reigned for about fifty five years. The actual amount of time is disputed, but a bad King should not rule for a long period of time.

There is very little known of Manasseh's reign. He reversed the reforms of his father, Hezekiah, and worshipped foreign gods, and he defiled the Temple in Jerusalem. Some learned scholars claim that he was responsible for the destruction of the Ark of the Covenant. His acts and deeds, however, have been excised from the annals of history.

We know that as a general rule the histories of Kings were recorded. That there is so little known of a reign of fifty five years is quite extraordinary. If it were simply that a King reigned for a long time if God favoured him, then God must have approved of Manasseh. According to the Old Testament, this should not be the case since Manasseh did not follow any form of exclusive worship of the LORD or any of His commandments.

The answer in the mind of the historian was simply to be silent over the whole matter and to record only the events of the Kings of which he approved. Josiah is a good thing, so we are told about him. Manasseh is not a good thing, so only the barest information is given.

The next notable event in the history of the Southern Kingdom of Judah occurred under King Josiah, ruling between 649-609BC. The wider political situation in the Ancient Near East meant that Josiah had a relatively free hand in his rule of both Jerusalem and the whole of the Kingdom of Judah. Assyria had never really recovered from the rebellion of the Babylonians, and they themselves, recently freed from the yoke of the Assyrians, were not yet a force to be reckoned with. Even Egypt was still recovering from Assyrian oppression. In this situation, freed from outside influence, the young King came to the throne.

His reforms were religious in nature. He enforced strictly monotheistic worship of the LORD and purified all the places of worship in his Kingdom:

> And the King commanded Hilkiah, the high priest, and the priests of the second order, and the keepers of the threshold, to bring out of the temple of the LORD all the vessels made for Ba'al, for Asherah,

> and for all the host of heaven; he burned them outside Jerusalem in the fields of the Kidron, and carried their ashes to Bethel.
> He deposed the idolatrous priests whom the Kings of Judah had ordained to burn incense in the high places at the cities of Judah and round about Jerusalem; those also who burned incense to Ba'al, to the sun, and the moon, and the constellations, and all the host of the heavens. And he brought out the Asherah from the house of the LORD, outside Jerusalem, to the brook Kidron, and burned it at the brook Kidron, and beat it to dust and cast the dust of it upon the graves of the common people.
> And he broke down the houses of the male cult prostitutes which were in the house of the LORD, where the women wove hangings for the Asherah. And he brought all the priests out of the cities of Judah, and defiled the high places where the priests had burned incense, from Geba to Beersheba; and he broke down the high places of the gates that were at the entrance of the gate of Joshua the governor of the city, which were on one's left at the gate of the city.
>
> II Kings 23:4-8

Another of the significant things that happened during the reign of King Josiah was finding the scroll of the law. This happened during the Temple repairs. It was delivered to the King and seems to have been the impetus for the reforms which he instigated. It is sometimes thought that this scroll was the book of Deuteronomy, but this is not known for certain.

The reforms instituted by King Josiah did not last. Subsequent Kings, according to the Old Testament, followed the sinful ways of Manasseh, and eventually the Southern Kingdom also fell. This time it was not the Assyrians, but the Babylonians who were the oppressors. Babylon came up to Jerusalem and besieged it. The Temple was sacked and Jerusalem was destroyed in the year 586BC.

> In the fifth month, on the seventh day of the month - which was the nineteenth year of King Nebuchadnezzar, King of Babylon - Nebuzaradan, the captain of the bodyguard, a servant of the King of Babylon, came to Jerusalem. And he burned the house of the LORD, and the King's house and all the houses of Jerusalem; every great house he burned down. And all the army of the Chaldeans, who were with the captain of the guard, broke down the walls around Jerusalem. And the rest of the people who were left in the city and the deserters who had deserted to the King of Babylon, together with the rest of the multitude, Nebuzaradan the captain of the guard carried into exile.
> But the captain of the guard left some of the poorest of the land to be vinedressers and ploughmen.
> II Kings 25:8-12

Again we see that later compilers find a theological reason for the sacking of Jerusalem. As with the Northern Kingdom of Israel, so Judah had not worshipped the LORD, but rather had followed the practices of the Canaanites. The LORD's judgement was clear and true. There were no grey areas; you either did or did not do what was pleasing in the eyes of the LORD.

Before it fell, the Northern Kingdom was a vassal of Assyria, or at least paid tribute to it. The Southern Kingdom had also fallen in a similar way to the power of this mighty foe.

The Assyrians had remained powerful under King Shalmaneser and his son Sargon II.

The Old Testament

The Kingdom of Judah saw the destruction of their northern brothers and bided their time. Backed by the Egyptians and Babylonians, Hezekiah, King of Judah withheld tribute to the Assyrian King. By this time the formidable King Sargon II had died and his son Sennacherib ruled in his stead. Sennacherib was not the man his father had been, and to add to his woes, he also faced a rebellion at home. His father Sargon II had defeated the Babylonians and united the two countries, Assyria and Babylon. When Sargon II died, Babylon rebelled and used the Kingdom of Judah as a way of overthrowing the united Assyrian/Babylonian entity.

Sennacherib was coming against Judah with only half an army and rebellion on the home front. Even then Sennacherib still managed both to ravage the land of Judah and to exact a great tribute from Hezekiah. He did not, however, invade and sack Jerusalem. A contemporary account by Sennacherib himself reads as follows:

> Because Hezekiah, King of Judah, would not submit to my yoke, I came up against him, and by force of arms and by the might of my power I took 46 of his strong fenced cities; and of the smaller towns which were scattered about, I took and plundered a countless number. From these places I took and carried off 200,156 persons, old and young, male and female, together with horses and mules, asses and camels, oxen and sheep, a countless multitude; and Hezekiah himself I shut up in Jerusalem, his capital city, like a bird in a cage, building towers round the city to hem him in, and raising banks of earth against the gates, so as to prevent escape... Then upon

> Hezekiah there fell the fear of the power of my arms, and he sent out to me the chiefs and the elders of Jerusalem with 30 talents of gold and 800 talents of silver, and diverse treasures, a rich and immense booty... All these things were brought to me at Nineveh, the seat of my government.
>
> Taylor Prism

This is an extra Biblical account of the plunder of the land of Judah.

According to the Old Testament, King Hezekiah succeeded in his campaigns against Sennacherib because of his faithfulness to the LORD.

Both the Kingdom of Israel and Judah had now been destroyed. Israel had been assimilated into the Kingdoms of the world and Judah deported to Babylon.

The time of the Kingdoms was at an end.

<u>The People of God in Exile</u>

History did not stop.

Far away in Persia, in 559BC, a man called Cyrus was born and through a series of dynastic struggles, he managed to gain the throne of the Persians and united it to the Kingdom of the Medes. He then went on and effectively conquered most of the known world. Crucially for the People of God, in 538BC he defeated the city of Babylon and brought the Babylonian Empire to an end.

Cyrus' foreign policy was radically different from Nebuchadnezzar's. Nebuchadnezzar had centralised all the elite of the conquered nations into one city. Cyrus did not. He sent them home under edict to raise tribute. Financially this made sense as the defeated nations could provide greater income under the leadership of the nobles who until now had been languishing in Babylon. It also made political sense for Cyrus could now leave his capital safe in the knowledge that it no longer contained the ruling forces of conquered nations just waiting for the opportunity to revolt.

With their ability to see the hand of God in all world history the Jews interpreted Cyrus' action as follows:

> Now in the first year of Cyrus King of Persia, that the word of the LORD by the mouth of Jeremiah might be accomplished, the LORD stirred up the spirit of Cyrus King of Persia so that he made a proclamation throughout all his Kingdom and also put it in writing: "Thus says Cyrus King of Persia, 'The LORD, the God of heaven, has given me all the Kingdoms of the earth, and He has charged me to build Him a house at Jerusalem, which is in Judah. Whoever is among you of all His people, may the LORD His God be with him. Let him go up.'"
> II Chronicles 36:22-23

It is God the LORD who is in charge of history and so it was His Spirit who was responsible for the release of the chosen people from the chains of captivity. The hand may have been that of Cyrus the Great, but the Spirit was God's.

This was the only way the exiles could come to terms with the great catastrophe.

Back in the time of Abraham, the promise of the land had been a sign of God's fidelity to the covenant. During the Exile the Jews had to ask themselves what this new situation meant for their God. The gods of the nations seemed to have triumphed. Was the LORD all-powerful if the gods of the Babylonians had taken His chosen people into captivity? If the LORD's covenantal sign to the patriarchs had been the land, was the covenant still valid if the land had been taken away?

The resolution to these problems of identity and the authority of God was only formulated with a development in understanding the universal power of God. God could now take and use foreign nations and rulers for His purpose. Cyrus, although a Gentile, was the chosen one of the LORD, for through him, after the Jews had been taught obedience to God, the land was returned to them. The LORD had graciously given it back to them from the hand of Cyrus the Great. Cyrus was even called a Messiah, a chosen one of God, chosen to free the People of God from captivity in Babylon.

This is why so much material was recorded in the time of Exile. If we believe that the work of the Deuteronomists preceded the Exile, then it most definitely continued at the time of national crisis. Challenges to the Kingdom of Judah had given rise to a greater impetus to instruction in the law and the redaction (the editing) of history to reflect the theological situation. These challenges to the Kingdom were as nothing to the national catastrophe of the Exile. The work of recording history was an important factor in maintaining a distinct identity of the People of God. This history had to be accessible, visible and theologically understandable.

If this was the work of the Deuteronomists, then there was also the work of the Priests, or the Priestly Source. This source had a fixation on lists and genealogies and the importance of the priestly caste. We can see their work throughout the Old Testament. Suddenly out of nowhere lists and genealogies appear. Genealogies, of course, are of vital importance if one was trying to keep national identity alive. One needed to know who these characters were, where they came from and to whom they were related. One needs to know what the land was like, who it had belonged to and what had happened there before. Finally, for the correct worship of God, the lack of which had led to the destruction of the Kingdoms in the first place, the rites and rituals had to be recorded and preserved, so that when they returned from Exile the people would know exactly what to do.

The same problems could not be allowed to happen again.

The Return of the People of God

With the Exile the great history books of the Old Testament came to an end: I and II Samuel, I and II Kings, with their parallels in I and II Chronicles. The history was taken up again by Ezra and Nehemiah.

The history books record that Cyrus allowed the exiles to return home. The grandson of the last but one King of Judah was the one who led them back. Zerubbabel was not a King, but the governor of Judah. He led home, according to the texts, about fifty thousand men and women. The High Priest who accompanied the returning exiles was Joshua.

Soon the reconstruction of the Temple took place. This was known as the "Second Temple", the first being the one constructed under King Solomon.

After political skirmishes with the Samaritans (the successors of the Kingdom of Israel, after the capital had been moved to Samaria), the Temple was finished in 516BC and dedicated in 515BC. This Second Temple, however, lacked many of the cultic objects which had been a fixture of the Temple in the time before the Exile. There was no Ark of the Covenant, no Flowering Rod, and no Tablets of the Covenant. The Holy of Holies was no longer partitioned by a wall, but by a curtain. The theology and structure was fundamentally the same, but with the absence of cultic objects the presence of God had to be refined and rarefied.

Terms such as the "Name" or "Holiness" of the LORD were now used to describe the abiding presence of God. This was the way in which God now came to, and communicated with, His people. This transcendence of God continued in the theology of the Jews. The result of the Temple being destroyed along with all the holy objects was that the presence of God could not be confined to tangible and visible objects (if, indeed, He ever could).

It was not the old religion of the nations when the presence of a god abided in a statue. If this had been the case then the LORD would have been destroyed when the Temple had been razed to the ground. The presence of God was something which was beyond these visible signs.

As the Psalmist wrote "Our God is in the heavens, He does whatever He wills" (Psalm 113:11). If He is in the heavens, He is not here.

It is also after this time that the emphasis on angels gained ground. Their existence had been attested in very early writings, such as Jacob's wrestling match with the angel in Genesis 32. Their importance as representing the presence of God, almost as a kind of insulator against the divine, was a later development. God became transcendent and needed someone or something to communicate Him to His creation.

After the works of Ezra and Nehemiah and the dedication of the Second Temple, explicit history of this period in the Old Testament came to an end. The next historical works which take up the story are the books of the Maccabees.

The Maccabean Revolt

In the mid fourth century the Persian Empire, under King Darius III, was defeated by Alexander the Great. Through a succession of military conquests, all of the land of the returned exiles fell under Greek sway. This did not last long, for after the reign of Alexander, his empire was divided into four. The part containing

History

the People of God was ruled by the Seleucid dynasty (and for a brief period parts they were also under the section governed by the Ptolemys). This ran from 312-63BC.

fig. 1

fig. 2

Fig. 1: the Cyrus Cylinder dating from 539-530BC. Held in the British Museum. It is written in Akkadian cuneiform (fig. 2) and relates the conquest of the Babylonian Empire by Cyrus the Great.

Even though particular Kings and rulers came and went, it was characterised by an elevation of the Greek civilisation and Greek culture and practices. It was in this period, as we have seen above, that the Septuagint was produced in Alexandria under Ptolemy II Philadelphus (285-246BC).

None of these overlords seems to have caused many problems until the rise of Antiochus IV Epiphanes who ruled from 175-164BC. It is tempting to paint Antiochus IV Epiphanes as the originator of the revolt which took place in the mid second century BC, but its roots lie before his rise to power.

As has been said, there was a strong force in the land which prized all things Greek. We know from the first book of the Maccabees that gymnasia had been built in the land and the status of the High Priest had become corrupt, secured by bribes and deceit. Furthermore, the Jews ceased to follow the covenant that God had made with them. They set up strange altars and even "removed their marks of circumcision" (I Maccabees 1:15).

Around 170BC, Antiochus IV Epiphanes was waging war in Egypt and, while the major power force was away, a Jew named Jason removed the High Priest Menelaus. Menelaus had previously replaced the same Jason as High Priest. Menelaus was a supporter of Antiochus IV Epiphanes and Jason favoured the Syrians, who in turn were opposed to Antiochus. When Antiochus realised what had happened he returned in 167BC and sacked Jerusalem and the Temple:

> When these happenings were reported to the King, he thought that Judea was in revolt. Raging like a wild animal, he set out from Egypt and took Jerusalem by storm. He ordered his soldiers to cut down without mercy those whom they met and to slay those who took refuge in their houses. There was a massacre of young and old, a killing of women and children, a slaughter of virgins and infants. In the space of three days, eighty thousand were lost, forty thousand meeting a violent death, and the same number being sold into slavery.
>
> II Maccabees 5:11-14

Antiochus decided that the fundamental reason for this revolt was the Jewish faith and that the only way to counter this threat to his rule was to promote ruthlessly the hellenizing (that is, the Greek) influence and at the same time to outlaw Judaism.

In a series of measures he forbade the practice of all things Jewish. He banned the sacrifices. He banned the religious festivals and even the observance of the Sabbath. He banned the practice of circumcision. The Jews were forced to worship Greek gods and to that end altars to Zeus were erected, even in the Temple in Jerusalem. Sacrifices of unclean animals were offered in the holy places. It was a capital offence to possess copies of the Sacred Scriptures.

This decree so incensed some Jewish communities, though one has to say not all, that a revolt broke out in a small rural backwater called Modiin. Its instigator was not a major political player, but a country priest called Mattathias. That the revolt did not break out in the centre of Jerusalem may be a sign of the power of the political overlords, or the reality of how far many Jews had taken this process of hellenization on board. Mattathias refused to offer sacrifice to the foreign gods and when one of his priestly countrymen, influenced by the Greeks, offered to come forward and do it for him, Mattathias was so incensed that he killed the man. His family of five sons fled into the wilderness and there, for a number of years, waged a guerrilla war against Antiochus.

These wars continued until one of Mattathias' sons, Judas, entered Jerusalem and imposed another brother, Jonathan Maccabeus, as High Priest. The Temple was rededicated and cleansed.

This was tolerated because when Judas was entering Jerusalem and the Syrians were preparing to send an army of re-occupation, Antiochus IV Epiphanes died. In the power vacuum, a compromise was reached and religious freedom allowed.

Eventually, under the last of the Maccabees in 142BC Simon Maccabeus made a political agreement with the Syrian King, Demetrius II, which allowed the Jews complete political and religious freedom.

This freedom lasted until Pompey, the great Roman general, captured Jerusalem. He subjected it and the whole of Judea to Roman control in 63BC. The rule of the Romans was to prove an end to the possession of the land.

Under the watchful eye of Rome, in 37BC Herod the Great became King of the Jews.

A bas relief from the Assyrain Capital Khorsabad of King Gilgamesh who searched for immortality. Now in the Louvre.

8

Myth and Legend

The historical works which make up the Old Testament are composite narratives. That is to say they do not just contain historical data. The farther from the historical action the more difficult it becomes to match up the description with what may or may not have taken place. As one goes back, it is no longer really appropriate to call this material history and so here we name it "Myth and Legend".

The terms myth and legend may often imply something that is not true. It is assumed that this is material has been made up, even cynically fabricated. This is not the case. The ability of the ancients to preserve stories is well known, and these stories themselves were frequently founded on historical truth, interpreted in a way which was meaningful for people at the time.

An example would be the interpretation of the appearance of a comet. In pre-history such an unpredictable event would carry a particular meaning. When the heavens were studied with increasing accuracy by the Babylonians the appearance of a comet could be plotted and expected. Even so, it was still thought that they could influence the world. As science advanced, these meanings become more symbolic.

If we consider the story of the Flood it shows us why myth and legend should not merely be discarded as ancient fairy stories and fancies. The world view of the people has to be taken into account. It is more manageable to think of a flood which wiped out all living things throughout the whole world if one accepts that the perceived world was not necessarily very large. It did not include the vast continents and peoples of the globe. It was restricted to the Ancient Near East. As a way of theologically understanding a physical event it is relatively easier to think of the area from the Mediterranean to the Persian Gulf being covered in a deluge than the whole world.

The story of the Flood is seen in all the major religious systems in the Ancient Near East. This seems to testify that it may well been based on historical fact. This does not mean that a flood historically happened, but rather that a terrible inundation took place which destroyed the land and killed the animals. Few survived. This may not be a universal destruction, wiping out all living things from the face of the earth, but may have been quite localised. As the story developed, it remained anchored in historical memory.

More importantly, however, is the way myth and legend used the historical basis and theologised it. Every account of an event in this period is shot through with the action of God. The people needed to understand how and why God acted in a particular way at a particular time. Myth and legend does this. For instance, one of the things the flood narrative does is give a specific theological meaning to the rainbow:

> Then God said to Noah and to his sons with him, "Behold, I establish My covenant with you and your descendants after you, and with every living creature that is with you, the birds, the cattle, and every beast of the earth with you, as many as came out of the ark. I establish My covenant with you, that never again shall all flesh be cut off by the waters of a flood, and never again shall there be a flood to destroy the earth." And God said, "This is the sign of the covenant which I make between Me and you and every living creature that is with you, for all future generations: I set my bow in the cloud, and it shall be a sign of the covenant between Me and the earth."
>
> Genesis 9:8-11

The rainbow is a natural phenomenon which may be observed in the aftermath of a storm. There was a myth of a great storm lasting many days which covered the whole world and which destroyed all living things. Living things still existed and the land was again fertile. So, if God was in charge of the whole world, then it was He who brought about the flood and destroyed all things. For some reason God had restored them. The unexplained phenomenon was the rainbow. The ancients had no way of understanding the science of water vapour and the refraction of light. Nothing like the Flood had even happened again. God must have said that He would not repeat the action. Perhaps the rainbow, linking as it does both heaven and earth, was a sign of the love between God and His people after the storm: something which joins together the realm of God with the realm of His creation. We would no longer have to fear that the world would be destroyed because by the time the rainbow appeared, the storm had passed. The same thing would never happen again. The physical sign of this was the rainbow.

This is one way in which myth and legend can work. It explains the physical world in religious terms based on historical memories.

This falls into the category of aetiology. This is a story that describes a present reality. Modern examples include Rudyard Kipling's "How the Tiger got his Stripes" and "How the Leopard got his spots". The difference is that modern aetiologies are deliberate fictions designed to entertain. This is not the case with the aetiology of the Old Testament. They may contain entertaining elements and they may use humorous language, but their purpose is always to provide a truth which was beyond the reality that could now be seen. The only truth in "How the Tiger got his Stripes" is the present reality that tigers have stripes. The truth in the account of the rainbow is not just the observable and verifiable fact that rainbows exist and can be seen in the sky after a storm, but also the truth and reality of God's covenantal relationship with His people.

Another example of aetiology is the story of the tower of Babel:

> Now the whole earth had one language and few words. And as men migrated from the east, they found a plain in the land of Shinar and settled there. And they said to one another, "Come, let us

> make bricks, and burn them thoroughly." And they had brick for stone, and bitumen for mortar. Then they said, "Come, let us build ourselves a city, and a tower with its top in the heavens, and let us make a name for ourselves, lest we be scattered abroad upon the face of the whole earth."
> And the LORD came down to see the city and the tower, which the sons of men had built.
> And the LORD said, "Behold, they are one people, and they have all one language; and this is only the beginning of what they will do; and nothing that they propose to do will now be impossible for them. Come, let us go down, and there confuse their language, that they may not understand one another's speech."
> So the LORD scattered them abroad from there over the face of all the earth, and they left off building the city.
> Therefore its name was called Babel, because there the LORD confused the language of all the earth; and from there the LORD scattered them abroad over the face of all the earth.
>
> Genesis 11:1-9

This passage raises many interesting points. We can see that the story of the Tower of Babel is not dependant on its place in the Old Testament. This story stands alone. This is not the instinctive thing to do when looking at the Old Testament, but when considering certain elements of myth and legend, trying to fix them in a Biblical narrative is not always productive.

The activity of man is to build cities. This is common throughout the whole of the Ancient Near East It is both the activity of men and the duty of Kings. It is a good and righteous thing to do. When the LORD looked down from heaven, He saw the people and for some reason was concerned about this building activity. God almost seems challenged by it. The LORD's response is quite extraordinary. It is completely out of proportion to the building programme. We know that this section has nothing to do with the Old Testament around it, as there has been no prohibition on the building of towers, and this is the first time that God has had a problem with "reaching to heaven". In part, of course, the story shares a common concern with eating from the tree of life that one sees in the second creation account. If Adam and Eve had been left in the garden they could have eaten from the tree and lived forever. Both of these activities, building towers and eating forbidden fruit, could be seen as man over-reaching himself; trying to become like God. In the creation account, people would have shared a characteristic of God, namely to have lived for ever. Here in Babel, God's only concern is that if they succeed in building this tower, what will they get up to next? This is preventative action based on an external criterion. This is why the story only finds fulfilment in the category of aetiology. The end result is the main concern. People are scattered across the world and more importantly, they all speak different languages.

We take it for granted that there are many languages in the world. Even if there were only one ancestor language, over time it would develop in ways which would make mutual comprehension difficult or impossible. The people of pre-history did not have the luxury of such a historical overview. Although their perception of the world was large, it was still manageable. You could journey from one part to another, from Egypt to Babylon, from Asia to southern Europe, and from one city to the next. There was no sprawl in between. The city states could speak languages which were not understood by those around them and the languages of empires and nations were different one from another. Of course there was always some form of *lingua franca* for trade, but not necessarily for everyday communication.

Looking at this world then, two obvious questions come to the fore. Why were there lots of city states which are independent? And why were there so many languages? Although we take this state of affairs for granted, it did not really make much sense to the ancient mind. This seems to be the reason for the aetiology.

If we search for a possible connection to history we can look at the name of the city 'Babel'. It is linked to the term Babylon which in pre-history was a great city, though not always the largest. It also contained great ziggurats. Ziggurats were large stepped temples to the gods. These two elements could be woven into the story of the Tower of Babel, giving it historical flavour, without necessarily linking it too strongly to the historical city. The name 'Babel' was connected to the Hebrew verb "to confuse", "to confound". We do not know which came first, the verb or the place name, but generally in Ancient Near Eastern theology meanings of place names are given as a way of explaining the term, rather than the term explaining the name. "And that it why it is called…" is a good sign that it is not the case!

In the story there seems to have been a happy confluence of the verb in Hebrew, an ancient memory of a name and a great city which had tall towers to the gods.

These aetiologies are interesting as they are an example of how the Hebrews tried to understand the world around them. They used the ancient material that was available not just to them, but also to the people who surround them. Similar stories to the Flood are found in Sumerian literature, "Enmerkar and the Lord of Aratta", though here the building of the tower was to plead with the gods to restore the unity of languages. Common themes give rise to common aetiologies, or to turn it around, common themes arise out of the need to explain things by aetiologies.

Some elements of myth and legend within the Old Testament, however, may not be based on a possible historical reality and the struggle to understand the world. Let us take as an example the angel marriages:

> When men began to multiply on the face of the ground, and daughters were born to them, the sons of God saw that the daughters of men were fair; and they took to wife such of them as they chose. Then the LORD said, "My spirit shall not abide in man for ever, for he is flesh, but his days shall be a hundred and twenty years."
> The Nephilim were on the earth in those days, and also afterward, when the sons of God came in to the daughters of men, and they bore children to them. These were the mighty men that were of old, the men of renown.
>
> Genesis 6:1-4

This is a very confusing passage on many fronts. Who were the sons of God and how exactly was the spirit of God transmitted to the human race through the children of their union with human wives?

It may be tempting to seize on one element within the text, namely the limiting of a human life to one hundred and twenty years, and conclude that this is an aetiology explaining why we only live for a fixed period of time. The obvious problem with this statement is that we do not live for one hundred and twenty years. The basis for an aetiology is that there is an observable fact that one seeks to explain. Here there is no observable fact, for we do not live for that amount of time.

It may be that this story was a way to describe a stage in the process of shortening the lives of human beings. We can see in the Old Testament that the closer that one lives to the time of the expulsion from the Garden of Eden, the longer one's life. As time passed so the length of our mortal coil is shortened. This is not a definite rule, but rather a trend or feeling within the text.

Is this historically true?

First let us ignore the whole Biblicist agenda of 'Old Testament historical truth'. This is not a concern to us. Why are people described as living for many years longer than is normal at the time of the composition of the various strands of the Old Testament? Fundamentally we do not know. But we see from Ancient Near Eastern parallels, and also from within the Old Testament itself, that the 'Ancients' of whatever hue or type were bigger, better, stronger, faster than us. They were often described as being giants capable of great feats of strength and endurance. It seems to be a common way of viewing our ancestors. In modern times we assume that we are the pinnacle of all creation and evolution. To our forebears the opposite was the case. After all who was more blessed; the man standing now, rummaging through the earth having to offer sacrifices to God so that the crop would grow, or Adam who walked with God in the Garden of Eden at the cool of the day? Now man struggles to survive and his days are short. What could be better than to enjoy a long life and not be worried by the physical hardships that assail us?

Those who lived a long time ago lived for many years for they did not experience the limitations imposed after the Fall. Could the story be concerned with a stage between the expulsion from the Garden and finally cutting off man's chance of immortality? Adam and Eve had been thrown out of the Garden so that they could not eat of the fruit of the Tree of Life. This story could be a way of saying that there was no other way of living for ever. Even procreating with the sons of God would not work.

This is not entirely satisfactory. There is no initiative from human beings to procreate with the sons of God in order to live longer. It is the desire of the sons of God not the desire of human beings which is being addressed. The lengthening of life seems to be an unforeseen consequence of a discrete action.

As to the identity of the sons of God, we now assume that, in this context, the sons of God are angels. Of course as this is material from myth and legend it could well be an ancient strand of half remembered stories when strict monotheism and revelation of the LORD had not yet been made known to the People of

God. It could even be that this story concerns actual 'sons of gods'. Other religious systems of the Ancient Near East certainly included such figures. In times of pre-historical mythology such ideas would also permeate the people who would later become the children of Israel.

Where are we in the case of the angel marriages? Not very far, it has to be said. The sons of god may come from a time when it was thought that gods could come and procreate with the daughters of men. Or they could refer to celestial beings like angels.

Let us turn then at the Nephilim.

In the passage that we have been discussing, there seem to be two issues at play, though they may have been yoked together later. The first has as its subject the 'sons of God' - the angels. The second concerns the Nephilim. It may be that a link between the Nephilim and angels is implied. Perhaps the Nephilim were the result of the relations between the daughters of men and the sons of God. The word itself seems to be connected with the term 'giant' in Hebrew and indeed the Septuagint translates it as such. Of course giants appear in the Old Testament, such as Goliath, the defeated adversary of King David.

It is sometimes thought that these Nephilim were related to the Rephaim, a kind of pre-history race who inhabited the land before the Canaanites:

> In the fourteenth year Ched-or-laomer and the Kings who were with him came and subdued the Rephaim

> in Ashteroth-karnaim, the Zuzim in Ham, the Emim in Shaveh-kiriathaim…
>
> Genesis 14:5

These creatures were a race of giants with great strength. Instead of asking the question "did they exist?", "were they giants?" it is better to see in these fragments the tendency to place superhuman beings in the past.

It is an interesting question to ask if those who recorded the pre-history thought of themselves in any way better than those obviously physically superior beings.

In any case we have no access to this world. We cannot know who the sons of God were, or the Nephilim, or the Rephaim. They are lost worlds which are closed to us but whose echo exists in our Scriptures.

So far we have looked at two types of myth and legend. The first was aetiology, a way of understanding the world by looking into the past and explaining it. The second comprises pre-historical fragments and echoes to which we can have no real access.

Other fragments of myth and legend in the Old Testament can be connected to Ancient Near Eastern practices and as such are meaningful to us.

These are not so much myth and legend but rather common images which may shed light on the Old Testament. To understand them we can look at the texts and literature of the surrounding peoples. This example concerns the moment the Kingdom of the United monarchy is split between the Kingdom of Israel under Jeroboam in the north, and the Kingdom of Judah, under his brother Rehoboam, in the south.

We remember that under King David, the cultic objects were gathered together in the new capital in Jerusalem, and under David's son, Solomon, the great Temple was built, in part to house these objects.

The Southern Kingdom of Judah had its cultic temple in Jerusalem. The Kingdom of Israel had holy places, but no national shrine to bind the ten tribes that followed Jeroboam together. Then this passage occurs:

> Then Jeroboam built Shechem in the hill country of Ephraim, and dwelt there; and he went out from there and built Penuel. And Jeroboam said in his heart, "Now the Kingdom will turn back to the house of David; if this people go up to offer sacrifices in the house of the LORD at Jerusalem, then the heart of this people will turn again to their lord, to Rehoboam King of Judah, and they will kill me and return to Rehoboam King of Judah." So the King took counsel, and made two calves of gold. And he said to the people, "You have gone up to Jerusalem long enough. Behold your gods, O Israel, who brought you up out of the land of Egypt." And he set one in Bethel, and the other he put in Dan. And this thing became a sin, for the people went to the one at Bethel and to the other as far as Dan.
>
> I Kings 12:25-30

In the opinion of the historians this is just one more example of the apostasy of the Kingdom of Israel. So terrible are these people that they had set up false gods and bowed down and worshipped them. This is one reading, but we can ask what is behind the text, and why this action took place. This falls not so much in the category of myth and legend but in the common beliefs of the People of God. However, it is dealt with here as the images are ancient.

The choice of Dan and Bethel is not necessarily significant. They were cultic centres of the tribes, but there was nothing to connect them to the calves of gold before the activity of King Jeroboam.

So why is this incident so interesting?

There are two reasons. One is an unfortunate moment in history and the other is part of the belief system of various religions in the Ancient Near East and specifically the Canaanites.

The calves at Dan and Bethel immediately call to mind the moment of the apostasy of the Israelites in the wilderness. Moses had ascended Mount Sinai to speak to God and bring down the Tablets on which were engraved the Ten Commandments. At the same time this happened:

> When the people saw that Moses delayed to come down from the mountain, the people gathered themselves together to Aaron, and said to him, "Up, make us gods, who shall go before us; as for this Moses, the man who brought us up out of the land of Egypt, we do not know what has become of him." And Aaron said to them, "Take off the rings of gold which are in the ears of your wives, your sons, and your daughters, and bring them to me." So all the people took off the rings of gold which were in their ears, and brought them to Aaron. And he received the gold at their hand, and fashioned it with a graving

tool, and made a molten calf; and they said, "These are your gods, O Israel, who brought you up out of the land of Egypt!"

Exodus 32:1-4

The parallels with statements made by the priests at the shrines of Dan and Bethel are striking. Could it really be that they were trying to evoke the memory of the great apostasy against the true worship of the LORD? Were they really saying to the people of the Northern Kingdom that as a replacement for the worship that they could no longer participate in in Jerusalem, they could have a form of idolatry which had ended with the whole-scale slaughter of three thousand men and, just for good measure, a plague?

This would not seem to be an attractive proposition to the People of God in the north. Indeed this is so improbable that there must be some problem with either the text, or the reasoning behind it. Theologians have long thought that the figure of the calf had a great significance in the worship of the people who lived in the land which the Israelites were going to occupy and thus, by extension to themselves.

Let us make this a little more clear. According to the internal logic of the Old Testament, it would have been well nigh impossible for the Tribes of the Northern Kingdom to have put up two golden calves, one in Bethel and one in Dan, and proclaim them to be the gods who led the people from the land of Egypt. The only comparable image that they had, according to the historical narrative of the Old Testament, was that of the terrible idolatry of Aaron. Suddenly to resurrect this image would not have united the Tribes; indeed it would have done the direct opposite. The last time the golden calves had come up against the LORD terrible consequences had taken place. There is no way that the people would risk that again.

The image presented must have been positive. A worthy alternative to Jerusalem must have been given to them. It is only the historians who have a problem with this. The people seem to have taken to it quite naturally.

It may be said that they took to it too naturally. There are, broadly, two explanations. The first is that the imagery, technically the iconography, of the LORD was a calf or a bull. Under this hypothesis, when the Israelites pictured the LORD they pictured a bull. To the ancients the gods needed tangible forms. This could be anything, from a statue to a fertility symbol, such as a cultic pole. It could be a symbol of the sun or the moon, or it could be an animal. This first explanation is that the symbol of the LORD was a bull or a calf. When Jeroboam set up the two golden calves he was buying into the symbolism of the LORD. The LORD was seen as a bull, so to provide a new focus for the worship of the God of the Tribes one simply made a new statue. In this theory the worship of the LORD which stressed the absolute prohibition of any images was much later, and in the ninth century it was not an issue. The people would take to it because it was not novel.

This view, though simple, goes against the whole of the tradition of the Old Testament. There was no image and indeed no object, even including the Ark of the Covenant, that was the totality of the presence of the LORD. The fact that there were ongoing prohibitions against making images may well point to the fact that the common people desired an image, but never that this practice was sanctioned.

The alternative to this first view is a little more circuitous. We know that the main god of the Canaanites was El, an ancient deity who ruled more by reputation than power. The power among the Canaanite gods was wielded by Ba'al, the god of thunder. As the one who manipulated thunder and storms, Ba'al was extremely influential as it was due to his intervention or inactivity that crops could flourish or fail.

We know that there was a continual threat to the worship of the LORD throughout the Old Testament and this was due in large part to the attractions of Ba'al and his consort Athirat/Asherah, a fertility goddess. It was to her that the notorious raisin cakes were offered on the High Places, contributing to the condemnation of countless Old Testament Kings.

If the entrance to the Promised Land took place as the Old Testament states, then this really was a terrible betrayal of the LORD. He had saved His people and brought them out of Egypt to the place where He was to settle them and they showed their appreciation by following the heathen gods of the nations.

If, however, the entrance to the land was either more gradual or only carried out by a force which later accrued to itself all of the Tribes, then there were always Israelites in the land of Canaan who knew nothing of the revelations of the LORD to Moses at the burning bush. These may well have been following the god/s of Abraham, Isaac and Jacob which over time had been mixed up with the Canaanite gods. We know from other civilisations of the Ancient Near East that gods could be "imported" from one religious system to another.

Following this line of argument, the Israelites who entered the Promised Land under Joshua, son of Nun were only one section of the People of God. They had had the revelation of the LORD and had been saved and guided by Him, but this God was new to their relatives who had never gone down into Egypt.

Now we can see how two sets of gods could do battle for the hearts and minds of the people. The revelations of the LORD were exclusive, allowing the worship of no other deity. Through time this monolatry became monotheism. The worship of the Canaanite gods by the common people was a serious challenge to this.

Into this mix we can now put the combination of the gods El and Ba'al. The symbol for both of these gods was the bull.

Could it have been that Jeroboam was reaching back to an ancient tradition which was associated with the Northern Tribes and following the gods of the nations? His statement 'here are your gods' could well have been true if the people who had entered the land were not monolithic and if indeed they were the gods who had been worshipped by the people who had stayed in the land. Of course it would have been a lie, as these gods had nothing to do with bringing the people forth from Egypt (that had been the action of the new revelation of the God called the LORD) but it would have been a political lie for a political reason.

The Old Testament

The alternative to Jerusalem and the LORD was Dan and Bethel and the gods of the Canaanites who had been worshipped by some of the people since the times of the Patriarchs.

If this is the case then one can see how the people took to following these gods who were represented in images so alien to the worship of the LORD.

This use of mythological imagery, even if it is not from the explicit history of the people of Israel, can shed light on the Old Testament and try to explain how seemingly strange things can happen.

It is impossible to consider all of the material within the Old Testament that falls under the heading of myth and legend. Some elements, as we have seen, are simply incomprehensible. Some can be accessed under the heading of aetiology. Myth and legend can also be used to explain strange occurrences within the narrative of the Old Testament itself. But myth and legend can also be used to bolster religious and theological claims in a development of religious thought. Just as the historical sections of the Old Testament have a wonderfully hidden agenda, so does the re-telling of the ancient stories.

Let us look at the accounts of creation as a prime example of this. What follows is the second creation account taken from the book of Genesis:

> Thus the heavens and the earth were finished, and all the host of them. And on the seventh day God finished His work which He had done, and He rested on the seventh day from all His work which He had

done. So God blessed the seventh day and hallowed it, because on it God rested from all His work which He had done in creation.

These are the generations of the heavens and the earth when they were created. In the day that the LORD God made the earth and the heavens, when no plant of the field was yet in the earth and no herb of the field had yet sprung up, for the LORD God had not caused it to rain upon the earth, and there was no man to till the ground; but a mist went up from the earth and watered the whole face of the ground then the LORD God formed man of dust from the ground, and breathed into his nostrils the breath of life; and man became a living being.

And the LORD God planted a garden in Eden, in the east; and there He put the man whom He had formed. And out of the ground the LORD God made to grow every tree that is pleasant to the sight and good for food, the tree of life also in the midst of the garden, and the tree of the knowledge of good and evil. So out of the ground the LORD God formed every beast of the field and every bird of the air, and brought them to the man to see what he would call them; and whatever the man called every living creature, that was its name. The man gave names to all cattle, and to the birds of the air, and to every beast of the field; but for the man there was not found a helper fit for him. So the LORD God caused a deep sleep to fall upon the man, and while he slept took one of his ribs and closed up its place with flesh; and the rib which the LORD God had taken from the man He made into a woman and brought her to the man.

Then the man said, "This at last is bone of my bones and flesh of my flesh; she shall be called Woman, because she was taken out of Man." Therefore a man leaves his father and his mother and cleaves to his wife, and they become one flesh. And the man and his wife were both naked, and were not ashamed.

Genesis 2:1-25

The first thing to notice is the sentence right at the beginning of the passage. It concludes the first creation story. The world and all its array has been completed, and then suddenly we begin again with another creation story. The compilers of Genesis did not have any trouble with placing two entirely different creation accounts side by side. Indeed this would only be a problem if there were meant to be one definitive account of creation to which all people had to ascribe.

The two creation accounts are very different. The second, which we will discuss below, firmly belongs in the tradition of myth and legend. The first does not. It is a hard theological *tour de force* designed for a specific time and a specific place. The place is Babylon and the time is the Exile. As we have seen above, much of the Old Testament was reworked during the Exile to preserve and to bolster the Exiles' faith as well as to try to help understand how they could still have a relationship with God in a foreign land.

One of the results of this situation was the first creation account. It is probably the work of the priestly guild in exile and is a direct riposte to the culture of many gods, of polytheism. It emphasises that there is nothing outside God in any meaningful sense. All is without form and void. It is God who orders all things. Even the names of the sun and moon were stripped from them. After all, there were Babylonian gods and goddesses who bore those names. In the first creation account they were only lights which illuminated the world at the command of God. There was a justification for the seven day practice and a command from God that His people keep it holy. This would be a very visible way in which the people of Israel were different from those surrounding them. The work is orderly and stately, unlike the anthropomorphic and bloody creation accounts of the nations.

Such was the purpose of the first creation account. The second was very different. It presented God in a way which can be readily understood. He was not some omnipotent being who spoke and it was so. In this He bore more in common with the gods of the Ancient Near East. For this reason if for no other, we can see that this second creation account is older than the first. It is more gutsy and poetic. The images are fresher and more human.

In this creation account we can get rid of certain elements which we have discussed before. The aetiological elements can be readily identified. One can almost imagine a group of children sitting around their mother asking why she had to leave her family and come and live with their father's family. The answer she gave could well have been that included within the creation account. Not only does it provide an explanation of a present day reality, it also places it in the realm of a divine command and the ordering of the universe.

In the two creation stories we can see elements from the Ancient Near East. Some are widely different, some quite similar. For example in *Enuma Elish*, the Babylonian Creation Epic, man is created from blood and his purpose is to do the work of the gods. The human beings in the *Atrahasis* Creation Epic are men made of clay.

Although many other specific details may be similar, the whole thrust of the creation epics from other religions is different from the second creation story in the book of Genesis. The latter stands alone, while in the other Ancient Near Eastern tales the creation of man is simply one aspect of a story of the wars or dealings of the gods. If anything, man is only a work horse for the gods. The epics are not primarily about the creation of human beings. The second creation epic differs from this as it is concerned above all with the creation of people and their human condition.

This is not the place for a detailed exposition of the passage, but certain mythological themes are easy to identify. The first is the creation of man from the dust of the earth. As has just been said this detail is not uncommon in the Ancient Near East. It indentifies the passage as an early work. The relationship between the creature and God also reflects this. There are no formalities and there is no real idea of the transcendence of God. The relationship is immediate. This is one of the features of early religious traditions.

The supremacy of God over all of creation is shown but not stressed. In the Priestly account we are left in no doubt that it is God that created all things. In the second we are aware of it, but the story is not directly concerned with that detail. The second story is about the creation of man and woman, the reality of death and the prohibition of immortality.

In the second part of this creation story a number of trees take centre stage. There are two; the Tree of Life and the Tree of the Knowledge of Good and Evil. The story centres first on the Tree of the Knowledge of Good and Evil. It is the fruit of this tree that the man and woman are forbidden to eat. The prohibition is made by God:

> And God said, "You shall not eat of the fruit of the tree which is in the midst of the garden, neither shall you touch it, lest you die."
> But the serpent said to the woman, "You will not die. For God knows that when you eat of it your eyes will be opened, and you will be like God, knowing good and evil."
>
> Genesis 3:3-5

One can see immediately that there are two different reasons given. First by God, that the eating of this fruit will bring death. Second by the serpent who says that it will make the people like God. We do not know what kind of knowledge this is, and have no real parallels within the Ancient Near East to help us. There has been much speculation as to what this knowledge may have been that Satan was offering access to, but we simply do not know. The consequence is the same, namely disobedience of God's command. Aetiologies then occur. This is why death is in the world. This is why man's labour is hard and women's labour pains so great. It also explains the strange appearance of serpents and their seeming antagonism to mankind.

At the end of the story Adam and Eve are expelled from the Garden so that they may not gain immortality:

> Then the LORD God said, "Behold, the man has become like one of Us, knowing good and evil; and now, lest he put forth his hand and take also of the tree of life, and eat, and live for ever" therefore the

> LORD God sent him forth from the garden of Eden,
> to till the ground from which he was taken.
>
> Genesis 3:22-23

In passing it is worth noting that the serpent seems to have been right and eating the fruit from the Tree of the Knowledge of Good and Evil did make Adam and Eve something like God.

They are expelled to stop them living for ever. This final theme is also found in other myths. There is a common search for immortality. It usually comes about by dissatisfaction with the things of this world and a yearning to avoid the forces of death. This is seen clearly in the "Epic of Gilgamesh". During many adventures the hero Gilgamesh searched for a plant that would give him immortality. Having at last found it, it was snatched from him at the last moment.

The search for eternal life is a part of the human condition. We should not therefore be surprised that such themes are found in the Genesis creation story.

There are several oddities associated with the creation story. First the name of God is a compound. It is "the LORD God". The Tetragrammaton is added to the term for God. In English this does not really strike us, but it does not often happen in the Old Testament. This has led some to think that here in the beginning of Genesis we do not have two creation stories, but rather three; the second story being made up of two traditions which have been welded together. This would make sense of the compound name for God. As the two names for God in Source Theory are used to designate two different strands within the Old

Testament, it could be that creation stories were from "J" and "E". It may also be that one creation story was concerned with the Tree of the Knowledge of Good and Evil, and the other was concerned with issues of immortality and the Tree of Life.

This is just speculation, but it does add richness to the account of creation. It is not about just one aspect of man, but rather encompasses many things. Here myth and legend exists on several layers. In a way it is an extended aetiology because it does not just describe one thing in our history or present reality, but rather tries to sum up man's predicament as a whole. It speaks of our searching for a lost union with God and our yearning for the closeness which existed as we walked with Him in the eve of the day. It tells of our alienation not just from God but also from the whole of creation. Finally it speaks of alienation within ourselves, the fear of death and the need for immortality.

In this very brief look at the material in the Old Testament called myth and legend we have seen that some is lost in pre-history. Other stories have been woven afresh by later generations into historical narrative or theological explanations.

Myth and legend contain the ancient earthy elements of the Old Testament. It has some of the most vivid and beautiful images used in the Bible. It sticks in our minds as it did the minds of our brother and sisters in their ancient faith and it nourishes us as it did them.

9

Prophecy

In the Old Testament we tend to identify the prophets and prophecy with the Prophetic Books. These are divided into the Major Prophets: Isaiah, Jeremiah (including Lamentations), Ezekiel and Daniel; and Minor Prophets: Hosea, Joel, Amos, Obadiah, Jonah, Micah, Nahum, Habakkuk, Zephaniah, Haggai, Zechariah and Malachi. Prophecy, however, is more than the written material that we possess in the Old Testament.

Of course, there is a reason why these particular prophets remain and why their words were recorded and preserved for generations but they do not sum up the whole of the work of the prophets. Even a cursory reading of the Old Testament reveals this.

Let us look first at the ancient prophets and their methods. Then we shall consider the prophets whose actions are recorded but who do not have the status of a prophetical 'Book'. Finally we will look at the canonical prophets (the ones preserved in the "canon" of the Old Testament).

"Prophecy" in modern day usage is quite specific. It deals with the future. A prophetic utterance is one which foretells what is going to happen. This prophecy may be based on a sound appraisal of the facts, but the thrust is neither historical nor current. A prophecy is not an account of what has happened or what is happening at the moment. It is to do with what will happen.

Indeed, in common with this current view, ancient Old Testament prophecy was similarly concerned with the future.

There were many ways in which prophets prophesied. The prophecy could come about through dreams or visions; through altered states or mass hysteria. The will of God for the future could be divined through nature or specific objects. All of these prophetic practices were found throughout the Ancient Near East and the people of God used similar methods.

In Hebrew the word for a prophet is a *nabî'*. It is likely that the root meaning of this word has something to do with speaking or uttering. This fits in with the prophet being a spokesman for God, a channel for divine communication. This is why Moses thought that he could not possibly take the message of the LORD to Pharaoh. He could not be the spokesman for the LORD because he had a speech impediment. He could not be a prophet because he could not speak with clarity:

> Oh, my Lord, I am not eloquent, either heretofore or since Thou hast spoken to Thy servant; but I am slow of speech and of tongue.
>
> Exodus 4:10

Nabî', however, was not the only word which was used for a prophet. Other words are *ro'eh* and *hozeh*. These were not concerned with being God's mouthpiece but were more concerned with the manner of prophecy, specifically that of "seeing". The Old Testament implies that there was a progression in the term used for a prophet:

> Formerly in Israel, when a man went to inquire of God, he said, "Come, let us go to the seer [*ro'eh*]"; for he who is now called a prophet [*nabî'*] was formerly called a seer [*ro'eh*].
>
> I Samuel 9:9

This may have come about either because those skilled in being seers were dying out and the *nabî'* were taking their place, or because the practices of the seers were being discouraged and the *nabî'* were a source of prophecy that could be trusted.

So how would these seers see? Throughout the ancient world prophecy was associated with the interpretation of signs. This may have been anything from the flight of birds to the star gazing of the Babylonians. This type of prophecy seems to involve the prediction of the future by the interpretation of earthly phenomena. Perhaps there is an echo of this in an incident between Isaiah and Hezekiah. It is not so much a vision as a theological interpretation of an earthly action:

> And Hezekiah said to Isaiah, "What shall be the sign that the LORD will heal me, and that I shall go up to the house of the LORD on the third day?" And Isaiah said, "This is the sign to you from the LORD,

> that the LORD will do the thing that He has promised: shall the shadow go forward ten steps, or go back ten steps?" And Hezekiah answered, "It is an easy thing for the shadow to lengthen ten steps; rather let the shadow go back ten steps." And Isaiah the prophet cried to the LORD; and He brought the shadow back ten steps, by which the sun had declined on the dial of Ahaz.
>
> II Kings 20:8-11

As well as visions and dreams, these early prophets looked for the visions in the world around them.

Prophecy through dreams was a common way God communicated with individuals. Let us consider Jacob's dream of the ladder:

> And he [Jacob] dreamed that there was a ladder set up on the earth, and the top of it reached to heaven; and behold, the angels of God were ascending and descending on it! And behold, the LORD stood above it and said, "I am the LORD, the God of Abraham your father and the God of Isaac; the land on which you lie I will give to you and to your descendants; and your descendants shall be like the dust of the earth, and you shall spread abroad to the west and to the east and to the north and to the south; and by you and your descendants shall all the families of the earth bless themselves. Behold, I am with you and will keep you wherever you go, and will bring you back to this land; for I will not leave you until I have done that of which I have spoken to you."
>
> Genesis 28: 12-15

This dream prophecy contains all the elements that one would expect. There is a vision of the ladder, and the ladder has a symbolic meaning for it allows the communication of the vision to take place. The angels going up and down are the messengers bringing back and forth the prophecy from God. The vision is not simply something static. Its purpose concerns the future, namely the ancient prophecy to Abraham, that his descendants will be numberless as the stars. God modifies this prophecy to Abraham when He communicates it to Jacob and now includes within it a prophecy concerning the land. The Abrahamic call is not just about those who come after, but also where they are to live.

Here let us include a word of warning. Like the rest of the Old Testament these prophecies, though ancient in part, are also subject to historical reworking. Even within the overall history of the Old Testament this prophetic vision of the ladder contains elements which are out of place. The revelation of the name of the LORD has not yet taken place when Jacob dreams. For this we have to wait until God reveals Himself to Moses on Mount Sinai.

Prophets were not just concerned with religion. Their place as mediators of God's voice was essential for running any society. Whether the question concerned the invasion of a country, what battle formation to use, whether to settle on the right or the left bank of a river, or when to offer a sacrifice for a good harvest, prophecy had a practical application. This form of prophecy is perhaps the oldest, for it divines the will of God in a simple 'yes' and 'no' manner. This is called cleromancy. In the religion of the

Old Testament there are strange elements which may have been connected with this type of divination.

One of the ways this cleromancy was performed was through the 'Urim' and 'Thummim' which are later associated with the High Priest's breastplate. The meaning of these words is disputed. In the Vulgate the Urim and Thummim are called the 'revelation and truth', and scholars have tried to parallel the words with the Babylonian terms for 'oracle and command'. None of this, of course, is conclusive, but the words seem to chime with the use of the objects, namely 'yes/no' divination:

> Then he [Saul] said to all Israel, "You shall be on one side, and I and Jonathan my son will be on the other side." And the people said to Saul, "Do what seems good to you." Therefore Saul said, "O LORD God of Israel, why hast Thou not answered Thy servant this day? If this guilt is in me or in Jonathan my son, O LORD, God of Israel, give Urim; but if this guilt is in thy people Israel, give Thummim."
>
> I Samuel 14:40-41

The situation had arisen because of Saul's prohibition on eating. Jonathan had not heard him and so dipped his staff in some honey. After this, beasts had been slaughtered by the people and then eaten. Saul wanted to find out whose fault it was, either Jonathan or the people. He called for the Urim and Thummim to discover where the guilt lay. In the Septuagint, the Greek version of the Old Testament, in a previous verse the Urim and Thummim were brought so that they could "enquire of God". There is no doubt here that these objects are used to find out the truth.

In the Old Testament they are mentioned in connection with the High Priest's breastplate, the Ephod. We do not know exactly what this article was or what it was used for, but ephods also seem to be connected with priests and prophets for finding out the will of God. King David himself calls for their use:

> And David said to Abiathar the priest, the son of Ahimelech, "Bring me the ephod." So Abiathar brought the ephod to David. And David inquired of the LORD, "Shall I pursue after this band? Shall I overtake them?" He answered him, "Pursue; for you shall surely overtake and shall surely rescue."
>
> I Samuel 30: 7-8

As time passed this simple form of prophecy fell out of favour and became associated with the practices of the Canaanites and was condemned as such by the LORD. Interestingly they seem to have continued up to and after the sack of Jerusalem by the Babylonians. They are even mentioned when the Exiles returned to Jerusalem: "the governor told them that they were not to partake of the most holy food, until there should be a priest to consult Urim and Thummim" (Ezra 2:63).

The prophets were not uniform in their relations with society. In some places they were bands of ecstatic wild men who live on the outskirts of the community. Strange things could happen when a man came into contact with such ecstatic groups:

> Then Saul sent messengers to take David; and when they saw the company of the prophets prophesying, and Samuel standing as head over them, the Spirit of

> God came upon the messengers of Saul, and they also prophesied… Then he himself went to Ramah, and came to the great well that is in Secu; and he asked, "Where are Samuel and David?" And one said, "Behold, they are at Naioth in Ramah." And he went from there to Naioth in Ramah; and the Spirit of God came upon him also, and as he went he prophesied, until he came to Naioth in Ramah. And he too stripped off his clothes, and he too prophesied before Samuel, and lay naked all that day and all that night. Hence it is said, "Is Saul also among the prophets?"
>
> I Samuel 19:20-24

The prophetic spirit, whatever it may be, possessed Saul almost against his will. The person's subjugation was so complete that they stripped naked and forgot themselves under the prophetic cult. The prophets were organised in groups and were not wandering individuals. They do not seem to be performing any specific function.

With all of these different types of wild prophets, it is easy to forget that the gift of prophecy was also used for national and cultic reasons. This may be traced back to no less a man than Moses.

This charismatic figure, through the revelations made to him by God, had led the people through the wilderness to the point of entry into the Promised Land. Moses, however, was not just a religious leader. In his dealings with Pharaoh he had also proved himself to be a competent political leader. Although the people of Israel were not formed into a political entity, they did possess an identity which would continue for centuries to come.

This would culminate in the United Kingdom of the Monarch and would continue through the horror of the Exile.

Towards the end of Moses' life, God promised that He would not abandon His people:

> The LORD your God will raise up for you a prophet like me from among you, from your brethren, him you shall heed... And the LORD said to me... I will raise up for them a prophet like you from among their brethren; and I will put My words in his mouth, and he shall speak to them all that I command him. And whoever will not give heed to My words which he shall speak in my name, I myself will require it of him.
>
> Deuteronomy 18: 15-19

The voice of prophecy would continue, and through it the LORD would continue to guide His people. Through this action God and Moses divided the manner in which the people were to be ruled. Joshua, son of Nun was to lead the people into the Promised Land, while the prophets, who the LORD would raise up, would act as a corrective to political or military excesses. In all eras of political history we can see the action of the prophets. They stand within the court as advisors, or outside the court criticising either the King or the practice of the people.

In the time of the Judges, before the monarchy, we see a female prophetess called Deborah. She married together the two strands which Moses had separated. She sat as a judge, and thus wielded political power, and she also uttered prophecy, thus speaking with the authority of God:

> Now Deborah, a prophetess, the wife of Lappidoth, was judging Israel at that time. She used to sit under the palm of Deborah between Ramah and Bethel in the hill country of Ephraim; and the people of Israel came up to her for judgment.
>
> Judges 4:4-5

Deborah wielded her political influence when she declared that it was God's will that the people should no longer suffer under the oppression of the Canaanites and consequently took them to war. In this period prophets could and did rule the nations. This changed with the monarchy.

Even though the Kings performed some religious function, they were not prophets. David danced in front of the Ark of the Covenant as it was brought up to Jerusalem but this was not a prophetic action. Prophets had been intimately involved with the choice and anointing of the Kings, but if anything, this separated the functions rather than united them. The Kings needed religious legitimacy. This became a function of the court prophet and gained increasing importance at this time.

We see in figures such as the prophet Nathan at the time of King David that court prophets held an extraordinary power to rebuke the King. As the voice of God, they could say things that no one else would dare to utter. This institutional aspect of the role of the prophets puts them within the hierarchical structures, yet outside them, for they could rebuke and criticise the hierarchy without being tarnished in the political realm. For a moment let us consider the famous case of the prophet Nathan.

Nathan was the court prophet of King David. His role was both political and religious. We see the political nature of his influence in the succession of King Solomon after David's death. He was not, however, just a political apparatchik. He was first and foremost a man of God, a spokesman of the voice of the LORD. He, and only he, could rebuke the King in the greatest matter that faced David. The King had become besotted with a woman named Bathsheba. One day he had been walking on the roof of his house and had seen Bathsheba bathing. He became obsessed with her. From this moment David broke all of the taboos in the customs and laws of the LORD.

He started by having relations with her in the time of her fertility. As he was not married to her, this would have been bad enough but it was compounded by the fact that she was already married to Uriah the Hittite. Having had relations with a married woman at the time when she could conceive, King David then tried to cover up his crime by bringing Uriah back from battle and giving him the opportunity of spending time with Bathsheba. It could seem that she had become pregnant by her husband. The plan did not work as Uriah was a man of honour who would not think of sharing a bed with his wife while a military campaign was being waged. David went further and realised that the only way out of the situation was to murder Uriah. He put him where the fighting was most fierce and then told his forces to withdraw, leaving Uriah to his death.

King David had conceived a child by a married woman and then effectively killed her husband after his deception had failed.

Prophecy

The Court Prophet Nathan reproves King David.

Then God spoke through His prophet Nathan. Nathan related a seemingly unrelated story of betrayal and theft to the King and asked him, as a good and wise ruler, what he would do:

> Then David's anger was greatly kindled against the man; and he said to Nathan, "As the LORD lives, the man who has done this deserves to die; and he shall restore the lamb fourfold, because he did this thing, and because he had no pity."
> Nathan said to David, "You are the man. Thus says the LORD, the God of Israel, 'I anointed you King over Israel, and I delivered you out of the hand of Saul; and I gave you your master's house, and your master's wives into your bosom, and gave you the house of Israel and of Judah; and if this were too little, I would add to you as much more. Why have you despised the word of the LORD, to do what is evil in his sight? You have smitten Uriah the Hittite with the sword, and have taken his wife to be your wife
>
> II Samuel 12:5-9

The King had condemned himself from his own mouth. Through the action of the prophet the judgement of God had been delivered. This public chastisement was the role of the court prophet.

Other court prophets existed at various times, though not all were as successful as Nathan. Nathan managed to speak with the voice of God to King David and also steer the succession to King Solomon. Others were not so lucky when regimes changed.

Jeremiah was one such prophet. Originally from a priestly caste, Jeremiah served under King Josiah in the Southern Kingdom during Josiah's reforms to the religious life of the country. Jeremiah had not been destined to be a court prophet but came from Anathoth in the country of Benjamin and later prophesied to the capital city and the court. His prophecies corresponded to the reforms which Josiah was initiating:

> "If you return, O Israel" says the LORD, "to Me you should return. If you remove your abominations from My presence, and do not waver, and if you swear, 'As the LORD lives,' in truth, in justice, and in uprightness, then nations shall bless themselves in him, and in him shall they glory."
>
> Jeremiah 4:1-2

Jeremiah saw that the land had been polluted by practices which were foreign to the worship of the LORD. If the people repented of their ways then they would be saved and protected by the LORD. This prophetic voice, of course, did not need to be in exclusively royal circles. It could have succeeded just as easily if Jeremiah had wandered through the country of Judah.

Jeremiah did not always enjoy the favour of the rulers of the day, and when Josiah died many of his reforms died with him. God's message through Jeremiah did not change, but its reception did. He was mocked and persecuted.

Jeremiah is well known for the style of his prophecy. We must remember that these prophets, even the major prophets in the Old Testament, did not write books. They did not commit their prophecy to writing. Inasmuch as it has been recorded it must have been the work of scribes or court officials or brothers in prophetic guilds. Jeremiah's forte was using physical objects to drive home the LORD's point. We see this throughout his prophecies:

> Thus said the LORD, "Go, buy a potter's earthen flask, and take some of the elders of the people and some of the senior priests, and go out to the valley of the son of Hinnom at the entry of the Potsherd Gate, and proclaim there the words that I tell you…
> "Then you shall break the flask in the sight of the men who go with you, and shall say to them, 'Thus says the LORD of hosts: So will I break this people and this city, as one breaks a potter's vessel, so that it can never be mended. Men shall bury in Topheth because there will be no place else to bury.
> Thus will I do to this place, says the LORD, and to its inhabitants, making this city like Topheth. The houses of Jerusalem and the houses of the Kings of Judah, all the houses upon whose roofs incense has been burned to all the host of heaven, and drink offerings have been poured out to other gods, shall be defiled like the place of Topheth.'"
>
> Jeremiah 19:1-2, 10-13

The memorable part is the tangible object. He took a potter's flask and he smashed it in front of the people to gain their attention and to reinforce his point.

Using such strong images in prophecy was not just the prerogative of Jeremiah. We see an extraordinary occurrence in the minor prophet Hosea. The LORD tells Hosea to perform a number of strange actions all of which parallel the deeds of the Northern Kingdom. The first is this:

> When the LORD first spoke through Hosea, the LORD said to Hosea, "Go, take to yourself a wife of

harlotry and have children of harlotry, for the land commits great harlotry by forsaking the LORD."

Hosea 1:2

If this is historically true and not just a rhetorical device, then it shows the steps that the prophets would take to carry out the LORD's command, even to marrying a harlot. As if this were not enough, the LORD told Hosea to hire a woman of ill repute:

> And the LORD said to me, "Go again, love a woman who is beloved of a paramour and is an adulteress; even as the LORD loves the people of Israel, though they turn to other gods and love cakes of raisins." So I bought her for fifteen shekels of silver and a homer and a lethech of barley.

Hosea 3:1-2

We cannot know if these things were actually carried out by Hosea, but they were most definitely recorded as if they had taken place. Hosea, like Jeremiah, used far more than memorable illustrations to impart God's commands.

Jeremiah's message was the same as the Deuteronomists, the school of theology which gained such influence at the time of Josiah; return to the practice of the law of the LORD and the LORD will save you.

If Nathan was predominantly a court prophet with a political role, then Jeremiah's focus was first and foremost a religious one.

Other prophets existed apart from the court and positions of authority. Among these the greatest was Amos. He was a prophet concerned with justice and was possibly the first of the prophets whose words were recorded and preserved as an Old Testament book.

In his prophecy he immediately placed himself outside the prophetic circles. He described himself as a herdsman and a dresser of sycamores (Amos 7:14). In some way, this gave his prophecy validity as it was not connected with political motives. This was important for Amos because of when and where he carried out his prophetic activity. He was called by the LORD to prophesy in the Northern Kingdom just at the moment when the Kingdom of the United Monarchy had split. The LORD called Amos from his home in the south to go to the north to deliver the prophecies and judgements of the LORD. We see now why it was important for Amos to say that he was not a political animal. He was not a spy or fifth columnist sent by King Rehoboam to sow dissent and fear in his brother's Kingdom. At the end of his prophecy Amos was accused of doing just that by the court priest of the sanctuary at Bethel, a man called Amaziah.

Amos' prophecy has three themes. The first is that the Northern Kingdom has failed to worship the LORD and must return to Israel's ancient practice. We would expect this, but it is not the only concern for the prophet. The other two elements are equally important.

The first is found at the beginning of Amos' recorded prophecies. His prophetic style was to lull his hearers into a false sense of security. He begins by condemning the practices of the nations of the world, especially those known to his audience.

Damascus, Gaza, Tyre, Edom, the Ammonites, the Moabites and even Judah all fall under the LORD's withering denunciation. They had all sinned and so the LORD would judge and condemn them. Then comes Amos' killer blow as he begins to deliver the eighth prophecy in the same style and speech rhythms of the others:

> Thus says the LORD: "For three transgressions of Israel, and for four, I will not revoke the punishment; because they sell the righteous for silver, and the needy for a pair of shoes, they that trample the head of the poor into the dust of the earth, and turn aside the way of the afflicted; a man and his father go in to the same maiden, so that My holy name is profaned; they lay themselves down beside every altar upon garments taken in pledge; and in the house of their God they drink the wine of those who have been fined.
>
> Amos 2:6-8

Amos' charge is that just as the nations had been judged by the LORD so will His chosen people be judged. The surprising thing is that although we expect God to be concerned with those to whom he has revealed His will, the idea that He will judge the other nations by the same standards is new. In Amos' eyes this God is universal, and His judgements take into account all nations and people. The nations can be judged even though the LORD had not spoken to them. We can see how this development came to its fullness in the work of the Deuteronomists in Exile.

The other element of Amos' prophecy is the reason for the condemnation of the Northern Kingdom, apart from their rejection of the LORD. This is bound up with the political situation at the time of Jeroboam. The Southern Kingdom, we remember, had been devastated by the Egyptian Pharaoh Shishak. The Northern Kingdom had prospered. Assyria, because of infighting, had been weakened and Jeroboam used this to reinforce the wealth and trade that had been bequeathed to the Kingdom by his father Solomon. This was the background to Amos' prophecy. The influential and powerful were taking advantage of their position to widen the gap between rich and poor. This was being done not just by fair means but also by trickery and deception:

> Therefore because you trample upon the poor and
> take from him exactions of wheat,
> you have built houses of hewn stone, but you shall
> not dwell in them;
> you have planted pleasant vineyards, but you shall
> not drink their wine.
>
> Amos 5:11

This social element in Amos teaching is not just because he is a do-gooder, but because of the very identity of the people of Israel. To oppress the poor and act in this way is not worthy of the People of God.

The prophecy identified the problem and the judgement was given; Amos foretold the destruction of the Kingdom of Israel. This prophet looked at the actions of the nation and held its leadership and people to account. If they would not change their ways, and they did not, then they would be destroyed.

What we see in the conclusion of Amos' prophecy is a vision concerning the end of this age. We often see such visions in the works of the other prophets. Some prophets have visions which show that at the end of this age or era the Messiah will come and there will be a great banquet of fine wines and succulent food. We will consider such things in the section on Apocalyptic literature. It is enough here to note that such visions do occur in prophetic material in the Old Testament, and indeed may be a development of it.

Other prophetic books in the Old Testament are the product of their time and place. Ezekiel is written for the people in Exile in Babylon. It rehearses why the Exile had happened and exhorts them not to follow the practices of the nations in the midst of which they find themselves. It gives hope for a return from Exile and a vision of a new and great Jerusalem.

Isaiah can be placed in a series of contexts, though this is more difficult than with the prophet Ezekiel. Isaiah is thought to be a composite work. Scholars think that it may broadly be divided into two sections, called proto-Isaiah and deutero-Isaiah. There seems to be a break in the work after chapter 39. Proto-Isaiah had been prophesying around the same time as Amos, but he continued for a longer period. The second section (deutero-Isaiah), containing chapters 40-66, seems to come from the period during and immediately after the Exile. This latter section speaks of Cyrus the exilic ruler and mourns the loss of the Temple. The two sections have a different feel to them, as one would expect if they came from these two times in the history of the People of

God. The first warns of what will happen if the people do not amend their ways and do not return to the worship the LORD. The second concerns the consolation and comforting of the people once disaster has struck. We must stress that this breaking of the book of the Prophet Isaiah in two is only a theory. There is a great unity within the work concerning language, images and themes, but the text lends itself to speaking to two different communities and times.

Towards the later period of the Old Testament, the work of the prophets became much less clear. The wandering prophets and those who advised Kings and rulers by means of divination were no longer tolerated in the land. Their practices smacked too much of the religion of the Canaanites. The great social prophets were remembered as figures in the past, but they came from a time of affluence and security in society which was never again seen in the Promised Land. The priests and advisors gradually took the place of the prophets. Prophetic works were still being composed but they became mixed up with other literature.

The book of the prophet Daniel is one such work. It purports to be history, and yet large elements are prophetic condemnations of the nations and the practices surrounding them. As a prophetic work it is not as clear as the earlier prophets. The language of condemnation is cloaked in apocalyptic images. From being specific to one time and addressing one people, it becomes open to interpretation for all times and applicable to all peoples.

In the teaching of our faith we believe that the last of the prophets was John the Baptist, but to all intents and purposes the role and function of the prophets in the Old Testament had changed so much over time that towards the coming of Christ they no longer held the position that was once theirs by right.

They no longer divined the will of God. Their role as social conscience was taken over by the priests and their visions of the culmination of all time were subsumed within mystical writings. Undoubtedly such figures must have existed throughout the history of the People of God in the Old Testament, but their deeds are not recorded and their voices fell silent.

10

WISDOM

Of all the literature in the Old Testament, perhaps the most intriguing is the wisdom literature. It comprises the Books of Job, Proverbs, Ecclesiastes (Qoheleth or the Preacher), the Wisdom of Solomon and Ecclesiasticus (Sirach). In the Hebrew Scriptures, and thus in non-Catholic Bibles, the Wisdom of Solomon and Ecclesiasticus are excluded. Other elements of wisdom literature are found in the Book of Psalms and in the works of some of the prophets.

Traditional wisdom literature is associated with the figure of King Solomon. We know that the Old Testament connects Solomon with wisdom. It should not be surprising if later wisdom traditions were ascribed to this historical King in order to give them legitimacy:

> At Gibeon the LORD appeared to Solomon in a dream by night; and God said, "Ask what I shall give you." ...
> [Solomon said] Give thy servant therefore an understanding mind to govern thy people, that I may discern between good and evil; for who is able to govern this thy great people?"

> It pleased the Lord that Solomon had asked this.
> And God said to him, "Because you have asked this, and have not asked for yourself long life or riches or the life of your enemies, but have asked for yourself understanding to discern what is right, behold, I now do according to your word. Behold, I give you a wise and discerning mind, so that none like you has been before you and none like you shall arise after you."
>
> I Kings 3:5, 9-12

That wisdom literature is connected with such an important figure shows that this tradition was prized and that it also needed to be anchored to an individual who could give it a specific authority.

Wisdom literature can be divided broadly into three sections. There is a synthesis of wisdom literature and Old Testament theology; there are aphorisms; there is a type of traditional teaching on the meaning of life.

Before we look at these subdivisions we must see what place wisdom literature has in the Old Testament canon.

Even before this, however, we must say that wisdom literature is of great importance in Catholic theology generally; not so much for what it says, but by the fact that it exists. The underlying theology is the same as that which we found in the beginning of the work of the prophet Amos. We remember that Amos was able to speak of the offences of the nations even though the LORD had not revealed His explicit law to them. The difference between right and wrong was capable of being understood by all peoples irrespective of their belief in false gods. In Catholic thought, this is called natural theology.

Natural theology states that through the light of reason a human being is capable of reaching a limited understanding of God and also knowledge of good and evil. It teaches that although after the Fall men and women were excluded from a direct relationship with God and need to be helped with the gift of God's grace, they still had the ability to perceive something of God and a basic morality. In contrast to this, in classic protestant theology, the result of the Fall was so extreme that human beings could perceive nothing at all of the nature of God or any form of morality; all must be explicitly revealed by God. This goes against the prophecies of Amos and also the essential nature of the wisdom literature. Natural theology is written on the human heart.

Wisdom literature is an example of natural theology in action. Although the later wisdom literature, for example the book of Ecclesiasticus written about 190BC, sought to put forward traditional wisdom literature in the context of both Jewish law and Greek philosophy, most wisdom literature seems to exist apart from any specific revelation by God. These 'specific revelations' can be summed up as the "Law", which we will consider later. Law has an importance because of the nature of the Lawgiver. The Law comes from the LORD and so has a defined place in the religious practice of Israel and in the Old Testament. Wisdom literature may overlap the Law to some extent but it neither comes from it nor is it dependent upon it.

If this wisdom tradition did not come from a direct revelation from God, where then did it come from?

This is an interesting question. If we take natural theology seriously, then to some extent the question has no answer. Natural theology says that the seeds of wisdom are sown in all places and all times. All cultures, under this argument, should show signs of a form of wisdom literature. Wisdom literature, not being dependent upon specific revelation, could exist in almost all religious realms and systems. The wisdom literature that one finds in the Old Testament comes out of the traditions of the People of God as well as from the nations with which they came into contact. If wisdom literature were tainted by a specific theology which was alien to the religion of the People of God, then in a process similar to the redaction carried out by the Deuteronomists, it would be edited and changed. Within the culture and practice of the Old Testament this should not come as a surprise to us. The nature of wisdom literature itself, however, means that if this process did take place it would have minimal effect, for the nature of wisdom literature is that it is not religion/revelation specific.

Some may say that such a view sets up a challenge to the LORD. They say that wisdom literature is a source of teaching that had nothing to do with God and as such is an older and purer strand of moral guidance. Those who wish to criticise or expunge the Judeo-Christian tradition can use wisdom literature as a way of getting back to something which was 'ruined' by the rules and regulations of the revelations of the LORD. Frequently such ideas are connected to new age beliefs in a kind of natural 'earth religion' which wants to change revelation and destroy patriarchy. Unfortunately wisdom literature is easily malleable and can be forced into strange new religious beliefs for reasons that will become obvious.

Within mainstream thought, however, this challenge to the revelation of God is nonsense. If God is active in history, then He has been active throughout the whole of history. This is the same God who placed natural theology in the hearts of His creatures, so that they would have a chance of salvation even without the aid of specific revelation. The existence of wisdom literature is compatible with the God of the Patriarchs, the Old Testament and Our Lord and Saviour Jesus Christ.

Some theologians have tried to link wisdom literature with Egypt. We saw in the historical section a few chapters ago, that administration in the time of King Solomon probably came from Egypt, and through the marriage of Solomon to one of the Pharaoh's daughters there would have been Egyptian influence at court. It would therefore be quite extraordinary if some form of Egyptian thought had not passed to the Israelites. Not only had they spent some of their history in the land of Egypt, but Egypt was also an influential player in the Ancient Near East.

We must be careful to avoid the simple whole-scale introduction of Egyptian wisdom literature into the Old Testament. The world of the Egyptian gods and goddesses is very different from anything else in the surrounding area. The action of the LORD in history is closer to both Canaanite religious belief and the religious thought of the nations to the East around Babylon, than it was to Egyptian ideas. Although sometimes strong influences are felt between the Old Testament and the wisdom literature of the Egyptians, there is a fundamental incompatibility between it and the religion of the LORD.

Let us begin looking at wisdom literature by considering the wisdom goddess of the Egyptians to see what light if any she can shed on the Old Testament.

The relevant goddess in Egypt bore the name *Ma'at*. It is difficult to say what came first, the goddess *Ma'at* or the concept *Ma'at*. In any case they have the same attributes. *Ma'at* was the balance and order in the universe. As at one time all things had been caught up in chaos, so the process of imposing order on this chaos was a constant act. It was not that chaos had been changed to order, but that chaos was held in check by order. If order were removed then chaos would return. This was one of the principle functions of *Ma'at*. Things had to be kept in balance: in the moral sphere, the political sphere and the socio-agricultural sphere. In many ways *Ma'at* was a series of rules, teachings or concepts which performed this function. One of the hallmarks of the Egyptian system of belief was stability and a resistance to change. If *Ma'at* was followed then there would be no change, and more importantly, no need for change. *Ma'at* was the glue which held all elements of the Egyptian society together. If the principles of *Ma'at* were obeyed there was nothing to fear. Because of this, some think that *Ma'at* was not primarily a goddess, but rather a series of foundational principles of society.

The Egyptians believed that at the end of one's life, the soul would be weighed in a balance. On one side was the essence of the dead person, on the other was *Ma'at*, symbolised by a feather. The soul was weighed against the feather. *Ma'at* was the counterbalance in the judgement of morally right conduct. In various Books of the Dead, the laws of *Ma'at* are summarised in a series of negative statements; "I have not...", "I have not..." as a kind of checklist or justification for the dead person. *Ma'at*, then, is not just a guiding principle but also a series of prescriptive laws which have to be followed so that the soul may pass over to the other world.

What has this Egyptian goddess to do with the wisdom literature of the Old Testament?

On one level nothing. The guiding laws of *Ma'at* bear some similarity to laws in the Old Testament, but only insofar as it is a universal truth that one should not kill people or defraud them or sleep with their husbands or wives. The concept that a law must be observed to keep chaos at bay is not part of mainstream Old Testament theology. But it would be foolish to dismiss *Ma'at* out of hand. Of course she is an Egyptian goddess and as such is totally alien to the LORD, yet the principles behind her, and even, one might argue, some of the images connected to her, are found within the pages of the Old Testament.

Let us consider one such image:

> O God of my fathers and Lord of mercy, who hast made all things by Thy word, and by Thy wisdom hast formed man, to have dominion over the creatures Thou hast made, and rule the world in holiness and righteousness, and pronounce judgment in uprightness of soul, give me the wisdom that sits by Thy throne, and do not reject me from among Thy servants...

> With Thee is wisdom, who knows Thy works and was present when Thou didst make the world, and who understand what is pleasing in Thy sight and what is right according to Thy commandments. Send her forth from the holy heavens, and from the throne of Thy glory send her, that she may be with me and toil, and that I may learn what is pleasing to thee.
> For she knows and understands all things, and she will guide me wisely in my actions and guard me with her glory. Then my works will be acceptable, and I shall judge thy people justly, and shall be worthy of the throne of my father.
>
> Wisdom 9:1-4, 9, 11-12

We can gather a number of things from this passage. The most obvious among them is that the personification of wisdom is feminine. Some have argued that because the word for wisdom in Hebrew חָכְמָה (*hokmah*) is a feminine noun, the personification of the noun would take on characteristics of the gender of the word itself. This, however, is not a general rule in Hebrew. Words with grammatically feminine endings are not endowed with feminine images.

There are a number of things that we can glean from this passage concerning wisdom. She was present when the world was made and to some extent had a hand in its formation. By following her precepts and teachings an individual may live in a way that is pleasing to God. Most interestingly, if one is looking for parallels with the goddess *Ma'at*, wisdom also "pronounces judgement in uprightness of soul".

A depiction of the Egyptian goddess Ma'at with her symbol the feather.

A simple reading of this section of the Book of Wisdom would seem to support a strong link between the Old Testament and the goddess *Ma'at*. This would be an attractive hypothesis, were it not for the fact that the book dates from circa 190BC. It is a long time since the Israelites had left Egypt. When the following chapters of the book of Wisdom are read we also see that the whole history of the People of God from the creation of the world to their salvation and beyond are replayed with the actions of God being identified with the actions of wisdom. This close identification of wisdom and the LORD cannot support a view that would place wisdom as a principle in opposition to God.

It makes more sense if we see this emphasis on the 'Wisdom of God' as part of the process of reconnecting God and His creation after the work of the Deuteronomists had been taken to its logical conclusion. We remember that one of the ways in which the Deuteronomists tried to understand the calamity of the Exile was by stressing that God was neither tied nor fixed to any object or building. It did not matter that the Temple had been destroyed, for God was in heaven, stronger and mightier than any thing that He had made. The links between God and His creation became strained and language such as the LORD's Name and the LORD's Glory came to mean His presence among His people. He Himself could not be present, but His 'presence' could be felt though His attributes. The Book of Wisdom seems a logical result of this theology. The LORD's wisdom and the LORD are one. It is simply His way of dealing with the world. There are no rival gods or principles to His creative power and rule.

If we look at the surrounding culture at this period of history we can see that it is dominated by Greek thought and philosophy. This depiction of wisdom is not too far from the Logos theology of some of the Greeks. This teaches that the 'Word', in Greek the Logos, was responsible for creating the world. If 'Wisdom' and the 'Word' are placed together, then the Book of Wisdom may have more to do with Greek influence than Egyptian, even though ancient images of wisdom may still exist from Ancient Near Eastern and Egyptian days.

We outlined above three divisions in wisdom literature; a synthesis of wisdom literature and Old Testament theology, aphorisms, and traditional teachings on the meaning of life. The Book of Wisdom falls solidly into the first category. Here we have a development of wisdom literature, which has been welded to the salvation history of the People of God.

We can also use the figure of *Ma'at* when looking at another of the subdivisions. Aphorisms are truisms which arise from everyday life. They are generally short pithy statements and contain a truth within them. They stick in the mind and so usually have a form or structure which helps us to remember them.

This type of material occurs in many cultures and societies. In Greece around the year 700BC an author called Hesiod wrote "Works and Days". It is in the form of a poem and is concerned with man's labour and his ability to succeed if he works conscientiously. It contains many aphorisms:

> Call your friend to a feast; but leave your enemy alone;
> and especially call him who lives near you:
> for if any mischief happen in the place,
> neighbours come ungirt, but kinsmen stay to gird themselves.
> A bad neighbour is as great a plague as a good one is a great blessing;
> he who enjoys a good neighbour has a precious possession.
> Not even an ox would die but for a bad neighbour.
> Take fair measure from your neighbour
> and pay him back fairly with the same measure, or better, if you can;
> so that if you are in need afterwards, you may find him sure.
>
> Hesiod - "Works and Days" ll.342-351

Aphorisms do not just come from Greek culture; they are present in all civilisations. All one has to do is stop and think for a moment and we can all conjure up an aphorism that our grandmother, or some other suitably aged relative, used to recount at the relevant moment. Such aphorisms are an essential part of the wisdom of the ancients and even a kind of folklore.

Hesiod's work, though containing aphorisms, is not identical with the wisdom literature in the Old Testament. Other works in the Ancient Near East are much closer to Old Testament books such as the Book of Proverbs. Here we may look at an Ancient Near Eastern text called the "Story of Ahiqar" or the "Words of Ahiqar". It dates from around 500BC and was written in Aramaic on the Island of Elephantine, sometimes ruled from Egypt:

> O my son! teach thy son frugality and hunger, that he may do well in the management of his household.
> O my son! teach not to the ignorant the language of wise men, for it will be burdensome to him.
> O my son! display not thy condition to thy friend, lest thou be despised by him.
> O my son! the stumbling of a man with his foot is better than the stumbling of a man with his tongue.
> O my son! a friend who is near is better than a more excellent brother who is far away.
> O my son! beauty fades but learning lasts, and the world wanes and becomes vain, but a good name neither becomes vain nor wanes.
>
> Story of Ahiqar Chapter II, ll.41-47

These aphorisms bear a striking likeness to some of the proverbs found in the Old Testament. There is no logical or sequential grouping of the sayings in the Book of Proverbs and neither is there an overall narrative. It seems simply to be a collection of aphorisms loosely bound together. In this it is similar to the Story of Ahiqar:

> My son, if you have become surety for your neighbour, have given your pledge for a stranger;
> if you are snared in the utterance of your lips, caught in the words of your mouth;
> then do this, my son, and save yourself, for you have come into your neighbour's power: go, hasten, and importune your neighbour.
> Give your eyes no sleep and your eyelids no slumber; save yourself like a gazelle from the hunter, like a bird from the hand of the fowler.
>
> Proverbs 6:1-5

Wisdom literature in the form of aphorisms seems to be something which crosses both national boundaries and generations. It is indeed a natural theology and can be seen in almost all Ancient Near Eastern cultures. If we do not have a record of it in any particular civilisation it is probably from a lack of historical record rather than a lack of wisdom literature from the country in question.

The third subdivision in wisdom literature is the traditional teachings on the meaning of life. Within the works of the Old Testament, the Book of Job and the Book of Ecclesiastes deal with the greater questions of human existence. Ironically these two works give directly opposed answers to the question of the purpose of life.

We see men and women in many places in the Old Testament asking fundamental questions. This may not be done in reported speech but it is visible by the material that is left behind. We have already looked at the second creation story and seen that in part it answers such questions as 'why is child birth so painful and dangerous?' and 'why is it so difficult to make a living from the land?' These simple aetiologies (description of how a present situation came about) cross over into the larger questions of life when they start to touch the fundamental material existence of man. Why is life hard?

Wisdom literature, however, moves this into a wholly different bracket. It does not look at life and ask 'why is it difficult?' rather it looks at life and asks 'what is the purpose of all this?' and 'why do evil things happen to good people?' It questions existence itself and the very meaning of that existence.

Both of the books of the Old Testament which deal with this type of wisdom literature concern themselves with fundamental questions. Indeed we may say that Ecclesiastes and Job pose the two questions in sharp relief. Job, who was a just and holy man, faces the reality of terrible occurrences in his life. Ecclesiastes asks if there is any point in life at all. As both books, however, are concerned with the fundamentals of life there is no great divide between them. To ask why evil happens to good people is to ask whether or not there is a justification of the things that happen on earth; and to ask if there is any point to all of this is to ask whether there is something greater than the individual which gives meaning to the quality of the life that we live.

Both questions would be tempered by a strong belief in the after-life. If there is something of us that exists after our death, then we can put up with the trials and tribulations that happen to us during this life, even if they are the most terrible things that we can imagine. After all we have been promised that "our reward will be great in heaven". The decisions that we make as we go through life will end up having an ultimate importance only if our final destination is determined by what we decide to do, for good or ill.

For the ancients and within the wisdom literature this is not quite so definite. At this point in the development of the religious understanding of the People of God there is no fixed belief in a meaningful individual existence after death. If there were, then the questions of Job and the Preacher (Qoheleth, the narrator of Ecclesiastes) would simply come from a lack of faith.

This is not the case, for they are real questions arising from real concerns in a world view that does not have a developed belief in a soul that can gain the joys of heaven.

This may come as a surprise, for we, in our day, readily understand and accept the hylomorphic union of man (that we are made up of a body and a soul) and believe that the soul will be judged at the moment of death for salvation or perdition. But the ancient Jews did not know this at this early point in their history. They knew that human beings were more than just animals and that they had something of God in them, some principle that would survive this mortal existence, but the belief in a specific afterlife which would bring bliss and happiness did not exist in the early thought of the Old Testament. This is a later development in understanding. Psalm 6 says:

> For in death there is no remembrance of thee; in Sheol who can give thee praise?
>
> Psalm 6:5

And the prophet Isaiah adds:

> For Sheol cannot thank thee, death cannot praise thee; those who go down to the pit cannot hope for thy faithfulness.
>
> Isaiah 38:18

There is a belief that something continues to exist, a 'shade' a 'shadow' of the individual, but it does not seem to be in a state that anyone would seek or look forward to. In the limited understanding of the Old Testament wisdom literature there must be some form of answer to these questions here on earth.

These two works, Job and Ecclesiastes, come up with different answers to the question.

Let us look at Ecclesiastes first. The Preacher takes a long hard look at the world around him and sees that there are great contradictions within it. He sees, among other things, the problems that Job will face:

> In my vain life I have seen everything; there is a righteous man who perishes in his righteousness, and there is a wicked man who prolongs his life in his evil-doing.
> Ecclesiastes 7:15

But it is not even those stark moments of challenge which cause distress to the Preacher. It is simply man's lot that brings him to the moment of revelation. This wisdom literature is simply about everyday life:

> I said in my heart, God will judge the righteous and the wicked, for He has appointed a time for every matter, and for every work. I said in my heart with regard to the sons of men that God is testing them to show them that they are but beasts. For the fate of the sons of men and the fate of beasts is the same; as one dies, so dies the other. They all have the same breath, and man has no advantage over the beasts;

> for all is vanity. All go to one place; all are from the dust, and all turn to dust again.
>
> Ecclesiastes 3:16-20

All work, all toil, all enjoyment is tainted by the fact that one day it will be taken away. There is no ultimate purpose to anything as we will all return to nothingness. All our deeds, our memory, our fame will fade and be forgotten. With this mind-set the Preacher offers the following advice:

> Go, eat your bread with enjoyment, and drink your wine with a merry heart; for God has already approved what you do. Let your garments be always white; let not oil be lacking on your head. Enjoy life with the wife whom you love, all the days of your vain life which he has given you under the sun, because that is your portion in life and in your toil at which you toil under the sun. Whatever your hand finds to do, do it with your might; for there is no work or thought or knowledge or wisdom in Sheol, to which you are going.
>
> Ecclesiastes 9:7-10

To put it bluntly; everything is pointless, so you might as well do something because once you are dead you will be able to do nothing! In the words of the Preacher everything is indeed "vanity and striving after wind" but better vanity than nothingness.

Depressing though Ecclesiastes is, he is not the only voice in the Old Testament on the subject of the purpose of life.

In many ways it would seem that Job would have much more to complain about than the Preacher. The Preacher's are just philosophical musings while Job is caught up in some bizarre wager between God and Satan (the point of which is never satisfactorily explained). He has had his cattle and livelihood taken away from him and worse even than that, all his children die. Even his good name is challenged as his 'friends' assume that it must have been something that Job had done to bring about this terrible situation. And the cruellest cut of all is that none of this is justified. There is no point. The only reason given is so that God can prove to Satan that people can be faithful to Him even in the most terrible of times.

This type of patient suffering literature exists in other cultures of the Ancient Near East. There are parallels in the Canaanite literature with the Keret epics. A King named Keret is deprived of his whole family, even though he himself is good and righteous. Keret sticks to his belief in his gods and offers sacrifices. His faith has been challenged, but he clings to it all the same. In Babylon there is another story called *Ludlul bel Nemeqi* which is similar to the Book of Job. It has an innocent man suffering terrible illnesses and physical torments which he cannot explain. Some of the language in this Babylonian story is similar in its graphic descriptions to Job.

The fundamental difference between these other works and Job is that neither of the others, and indeed none in any other religious belief system, can actually pose the questions that Job does. To do that you need to believe that there is only one God and that He is in charge of the whole universe. In other cultures apart from the People of God other deities can bring about misfortune. This is always a possibility in the stories from other nations. In Job only God can bring about the calamities that he is suffering, no one else.

With this in mind, how is Job's response different from that of the Preacher?

In Job the story is much more detailed and human. In it, Job addresses God and demands that He come and answers the charge that Job lays at His door. He challenges God directly and insists on a response. This of course is missing from Ecclesiastes. The response that God gives is not what Job was expecting:

> Then the LORD answered Job out of the whirlwind: "Who is this that darkens counsel by words without knowledge? Gird up your loins like a man, I will question you, and you shall declare to me. Where were you when I laid the foundation of the earth? Tell me, if you have understanding."
>
> Job 38:1-4

The LORD does not give Job an answer, rather He ask how Job could even think that he could ask the question in the first place. The majesty and might of God are presented to Job, and Job realizes that he was petty and foolish in both demanding an answer and expecting to understand the answer that God would give. Job retracts his challenge:

> Then Job answered the LORD: "I know that Thou canst do all things, and that no purpose of Thine can be thwarted. 'Who is this that hides counsel without knowledge?' Therefore I have uttered what I did not understand, things too wonderful for me, which I did not know. 'Hear, and I will speak; I will question you,

and you declare to me.' I had heard of Thee by the hearing of the ear, but now my eye sees Thee; therefore I despise myself, and repent in dust and ashes."

Job 42:1-6

The response to the large questions of life in the Book of Job is simple trust in the plan of Almighty God, even though one does not understand it and cannot comprehend it. Job's answer is starkly different from the Preacher's. There is hope and there is purpose even if it is hidden from you and even if you are incapable of grasping it.

Wisdom literature (a scholarly, not a Biblical term) is a slippery concept in the Old Testament, even though it is easy to identify it.

Wisdom literature consists of the timeless sayings that convey truth and it is also the whole system for summing up the work of God in saving His people. Even more than this it is the tool by which God's creatures can plumb the depths of their very existence.

Indeed, it is the fundamental rules of social life and personal contemplation, the balance that keeps us in check in relation to our world, our mind and our God.

Wisdom

'Moses mit den Gesetzestafeln' by Rembrandt, 1659.

11

The Law

If we were to ask people what the Old Testament contained, after mentioning various stories and parts of the historical narrative and perhaps remembering the names of some of the prophets, various laws would rear their heads. Even if the only thing that they remembered was the Ten Commandments (the Decalogue) they would have some idea that the Old Testament tells you what to do, and, importantly, what not to do.

Law fulfils many goals. It regulates society and provides security within a particular body of people. You cannot just come and steal my goat because if you do there are stated consequences. Law also regulates the relationship between groups of people and nations. How are we to behave to the stranger in our midst and the nation on our doorstep? The law tells us.

Most importantly it defines the relationship between God and His people.

Of course some would say that this latter function of law is not essential for the regulation of any given society. Law can simply be the agreed conventions of any group of people. If it is only an agreed contract then it can be open to change and flexibility because it does not claim any form of truth which is greater than itself.

The authority of the law comes from the law giver. If my next door neighbour issues a law that takes half my garden, the law has no power, because the law giver has no authority. If the government issues a law that takes the garden, then the law is valid unless challenged, because the law giver has the right and the power to issue the decree. Any appeal against the law can be twofold: the ability of the law giver to state a particular law, and whether or not the law in question comes into conflict with any other law which has been given previously. With the issue of my garden; does the State have the power to issue the decree? If it does, can that power be challenged? If it can not, then one must ask if the issue comes into conflict with any other law or principle, such as the right to possess property and not have it sequestrated unless for good and lawful reason?

Law, then, can exist outside a religious framework, but if it does so, then it has two weaknesses. First, it only has authority as long as those who receive the law believe that those who make it have the power and authority to do so. Second, there is no ultimate meaning to the law, for what is legal today can be illegal tomorrow if the law giver decides and the receiver agrees.

This system of law functions until statements of objective truth are made.

Of course, we are looking at this the wrong way round. Legal systems were based on foundations of truth before they were based on agreed common consent. To understand any system which is different from our own we have to work backwards and see why societies prized the law so highly, when for us it is only true if we invest it with authority and only follow it if we find it expedient to do so.

When a system of law in a society claims an ultimate truth, it can only do so because of the ultimately true nature of the law giver. We know that this law is always to be obeyed because it is given to us by someone who is always right and is acting in our best interests. The only law giver who fits this description is God.

Law in the Old Testament has an ultimate significance because of who promulgates it. It is God's law.

So what is the role of law in the Old Testament and when did it gain the importance that it obviously had in later times?

During the time of the Patriarchs it seems that specific laws were not an essential part of the ancient faith. It was almost a private relationship between an individual and God. God commanded or invited someone to perform an action and promised something in return if that person responded to God's invitation. The free will stays with the person. He is free to enter into a relationship or not. We can see this with Abraham:

> Now the LORD said to Abram, "Go from your country and your kindred and your father's house to the land that I will show you. And I will make of you

a great nation, and I will bless you, and make your name great, so that you will be a blessing. I will bless those who bless you, and him who curses you I will curse; and by you all the families of the earth shall bless themselves." So Abram went, as the LORD had told him...

Genesis 12:1-4b

This is not a relationship founded on law, but rather a covenant between two parties. It is to this idea of covenant that we must turn if we are to understand fully the Old Testament concept of law.

These covenants should not simply be thought of as stemming from the call of Abraham. This covenant with Abraham is, of course, fundamental, but it is neither the first nor the only one. The covenantal relationship between God and His creation began at the moment of the decision of Adam and Eve to rebel against the authority of God. As the natural relationship between God and human beings had been lost, it had to be restored by a quasi-formal arrangement. At various points of history and to various people these promises had been offered and accepted. In certain circumstances there was nothing even demanded on the part of human beings.

The specific natures of the covenants are very revealing. One would expect them to resemble law contracts, and indeed, they are often portrayed as such. This, however, is not the case. Let us look at the first covenant, between God and Noah after the flood:

> Then Noah built an altar to the LORD, and took of every clean animal and of every clean bird, and offered burnt offerings on the altar. And when the LORD smelled the pleasing odour, the LORD said in His heart, "I will never again curse the ground because of man, for the imagination of man's heart is evil from his youth; neither will I ever again destroy every living creature as I have done. While the earth remains, seedtime and harvest, cold and heat, summer and winter, day and night, shall not cease."
>
> Genesis 8:20-22

The fundamental difference between this covenant and a law contract is that there is no demand placed by God on His creation. The world does not need to behave in any specific way and there are no further controls or limits imposed upon it. This covenant is not an agreement; it is a statement from God of an intention of action, or, in this case, inaction. Never again will God act in this way. It is even incorrect to say that this covenant is between God and Noah, as God's decision concerns all creation. As such it has been described as God's covenant with humanity.

Chronologically the next covenant is between God and Abraham. This has been considered in the section above on history. In this covenant there is a reciprocal agreement. Abraham must do something, namely leave his land. God will then act, for He will make Abraham's descendants as numberless as the stars. We saw too how this agreement was subsequently changed to include the giving of the land to Abraham's numberless successors. In this covenant we also take account of the individual promises between God and Jacob (Genesis 28).

The next covenant is between God and the people He brought from the land of Egypt. This is described as the Mosaic covenant as it is presided over and mediated by Moses. This covenant has all the trappings of a legal agreement. Both parties have specific roles to play. There are obligations on God and also laws enjoined on the people. The covenant is ratified by a ceremony involving blood:

> And Moses went up to God, and the LORD called to him out of the mountain, saying, "Thus you shall say to the house of Jacob, and tell the people of Israel: You have seen what I did to the Egyptians, and how I bore you on eagles' wings and brought you to Myself. Now therefore, if you will obey My voice and keep My covenant, you shall be My own possession among all peoples; for all the earth is Mine, and you shall be to Me a Kingdom of priests and a holy nation. These are the words which you shall speak to the children of Israel."
>
> Exodus 19:3-6

The Ten Commandments are then given as the detailed rules which the Israelites must follow if they are to fulfil their part of the covenant agreement. The covenant is then ratified:

> And he [Moses] sent young men of the people of Israel, who offered burnt offerings and sacrificed peace offerings of oxen to the LORD. And Moses took half of the blood and put it in basins, and half of the blood he threw against the altar. Then he took the book of the covenant, and read it in the hearing of the people; and they said, "All that the LORD has spoken we will do, and we will be obedient." And Moses took the blood and threw it upon the people,

and said, "Behold the blood of the covenant which the LORD has made with you in accordance with all these words."

Exodus 24:5-8

It is interesting to note that although this covenant is early in the history of Israel, its form is quite sophisticated. It involves an explicit acceptance of a law which moderates and shapes the actions of the People of God.

The next covenant of note is the Davidic covenant. The LORD promises the following to King David:

> Moreover the LORD declares to you that the LORD will make you a house. When your days are fulfilled and you lie down with your fathers, I will raise up your offspring after you, who shall come forth from your body, and I will establish his Kingdom...
> And your house and your Kingdom shall be made sure for ever before me; your throne shall be established for ever.

II Samuel 7:11-12, 16

The Davidic covenant only reaches its full meaning in the period of Israelite history when they await the Messiah. This will be dealt with below in the section on the Apocalypse and the coming of Christ. In the context of King David and the LORD, the agreements between them do not mention any actions on the part of David. He does not have a set of regulations to keep or a specific command to obey. In fact, David's moral conduct is not one which could be said to come from God at all. It is not as if his behaviour has been influenced by being in a covenantal relationship with God. We saw above, however, that this covenant with King David could have been heavily influenced by later attempts to understand why he had not constructed the Temple in Jerusalem. God's part in the covenant is intriguing. It is firmly based in Kingship and describes the rule of the descendants of David within the monarchical system. We know that within two generations the Kingdom had been split and within a few centuries it had been reduced to a governorship under a foreign power. This illogical nature of the Davidic covenant naturally opens it up to a mystical interpretation. Historically everyone would know that in a short period of time the explicit covenantal promise could no longer be fulfilled, for the line of Kings had died out. Its true meaning must lie elsewhere.

The last covenant that we are to look at is an interior covenant with the individual heart:

> "Behold, the days are coming," says the LORD, "when I will make a new covenant with the house of Israel and the house of Judah, not like the covenant which I made with their fathers when I took them by the hand to bring them out of the land of Egypt, My covenant which they broke, though I was their husband, says the LORD. But this is the covenant which I will make with the house of Israel after those days, says the LORD: I will put My law within them, and I will write it upon their hearts; and I will be their God, and they shall be My people."
>
> Jeremiah 31:31-33

We also see this in the work of the Prophet Ezekiel:

> For I will take you from the nations, and gather you from all the countries, and bring you into your own land. I will sprinkle clean water upon you, and you shall be clean from all your uncleannesses, and from all your idols I will cleanse you. A new heart I will give you, and a new spirit I will put within you; and I will take out of your flesh the heart of stone and give you a heart of flesh. And I will put My spirit within you, and cause you to walk in My statutes and be careful to observe My ordinances. You shall dwell in the land which I gave to your fathers; and you shall be My people, and I will be your God.
>
> Ezekiel 36:24-28

There is an argument that this does not constitute a covenant but is rather a change in the emphasis of the theology of God's relationship to His people. We cannot say definitively if this is an explicit Old Testament covenant between God and His people or not, but we can say that it involves the restoration of a relationship between the Creator and His chosen people. It involves restoration of the people to the land, and it involves a greater appreciation of how the LORD wishes them to behave. It also involves action on behalf of the people. In all of these ways it looks very much like a covenant.

Why have we looked so closely at the Old Testament covenants in a section on the law?

The reason is that 'law' as a guiding element in God's relationship with His people, is not an essential part of the way He and His people are bound together. The bond is a series of loose covenants. The exception to this is the Mosaic covenant on Mount Sinai.

When people think of God's covenant with His people, they think of the Ten Commandments. It is assumed that God's relationship with His people is intimately concerned with law, but as we have just seen that this is not the case. How can this have come about and how are we to interpret it?

When we considered above the history of the Old Testament, with various strands of material being woven together under historical and theological influence, what became apparent was that the external pressures of geography or political influence shaped the way the Israelites understood God's relationship with them. Put starkly, the Exile forced a major re-think for the People of God. We saw that the actions of Old Testament pre-Exilic Kings were recorded and presented in a way which emphasised those who followed the worship of the LORD and denigrated those who followed the corrupt practices of the nations. We saw an increased focus on obedience to the explicit law, stemming from the time of King Josiah's reforms around 625BC. During the Exile, the self understanding of those in Babylon and the survival of their theology was centred on a redefinition of what it was to be the People of God; how they were to behave and how they were to avoid a similar calamity ever happening again. They understood that they, in some way, had disobeyed the LORD their God and as such they had been punished to teach them the way they should behave. Their faith had been shaken and their land taken so that when they returned they would do so with renewed strength and enlightened eyes. The centrepiece of this development in the religion of the people was the law.

It would be the reading of the law and the assent of the people that would seal over the horror which had been the destruction of Jerusalem. This would symbolise the new chapter in the history of the People of God. When they returned and the Temple had been rebuilt, the law was read:

> And all the people gathered as one man into the square before the Water Gate; and they told Ezra the scribe to bring the book of the law of Moses which the LORD had given to Israel...
> And Ezra opened the book in the sight of all the people, for he was above all the people; and when he opened it all the people stood. And Ezra blessed the LORD, the great God; and all the people answered, "Amen, Amen," lifting up their hands; and they bowed their heads and worshiped the LORD with their faces to the ground.
>
> Nehemiah 8: 1, 5-6

Here the relationship between the law and God's dealings with His people can clearly be seen from looking at such passages. The law as the defining sign of God's relationship with His people seems to be a later development in their relationship. The earlier we go before the Exile, the less importance it seems to have.

How can this be, since the Mosaic covenant takes place in the desert immediately following the escape of the people from Egypt? Are not the laws concerning personal holiness, which are found in the Book of Leviticus, from this same period? Are they not written by the hand of Moses himself?

As the understanding of the People of God grew and their ability to record their dealings with the LORD developed, so the

Bible as we have it came to be. Early myths and legends were written down to reflect how God had created His people. The history of the nation was fixed and interpreted. Prophecy and prophetic works were gathered together and recorded. In a similar manner the laws of God were collated and systematised. Laws concerning ritual purity were important in a place of ritual impurity. Laws concerning personal conduct needed to be stressed when personal conduct is threatened. This fits perfectly into the period of the Exile. We are not saying that the law sections of the Old Testament are products of an age which is totally different from the age in which they are set, but we do say that the Old Testament makes much more sense when seen as a development of religion and faith in the context of the nation's trials and tribulations.

If we hold to the theological development in the Old Testament outlined above, then it is after the Exile when exact ritual is most needed. We know that before the Exile the rituals and sacrifices that were offered were not in accordance with the rules that we currently have in the law books. Either people wilfully disobeyed them, or they did not know them. Either way the laws proved to be important when the rituals were threatened. It is only then that the people realise that their moral and ethical behaviour had influence not only on their own personal relationship with God, but also the national relationship with Him. There was no such thing as private sin. It broke the covenant, and the signs of the covenant; the land, protection by God and identity as His people, were fundamentally shaken. At this point, and only at this point, can law take on the importance that we see in the Old Testament.

Personal holiness was vital, so that the people would not be polluted either by the filthy practices of the nations, or by diluting their blood through mixed marriages. Sacrificial ritual had to be observed in the most minute detail for fear that an infringement might bring down God's wrath: even one which occurred through negligence! The roles of the priests and Levites needed to be fixed so that the worship of God was pure. And the people, on whose hearts the law had now been engraved by the new covenant, must, through dietary laws and societal practices, bear in their outward bodies the signs of the inward reality of God's covenantal relationship.

These laws are given an ultimate authority, for they, in the pages of the Old Testament, are spoken by the greatest mouthpiece of God, the prophet Moses. Never again could these laws be challenged or doubted. Never again could they be disobeyed. Their records had now been written. And the record stated that Moses himself had told the people how to behave.

We do not know if Moses dictated the laws that the *Torah*, the first five Books of the Bible. Perhaps some of the individual laws date back to him. What we do know is that they fit well into the time of the Exile, many centuries after Moses' death.

As a conclusion to this section on law in the Old Testament, let us consider the most famous laws of all: the Ten Commandments.

Law

The Ten Commandments in Hebrew are known as the "Ten Words". In Greek this was translated as Δεκαλογος from which we get the term "Decalogue". They are recorded in Exodus 20 and Deuteronomy 5. They are the commandments which were given to Moses on Mount Sinai (in some passages referred to as Mount Horeb). As there are no verse divisions in the original Hebrew text, the Ten Commandments have been assigned differently throughout history. We follow the Hebrew division which was recorded by Saint Augustine in his work "Questions of Exodus" (*"Quæstionum in Heptateuchum libri VII"*, Bk. II, Question lxxi). They are as follows:

1. I am the LORD your God Who brought you from the land of Egypt. You shall have no other Gods apart from Me, nor shall you make any graven images.
2. You shall not take the name of the LORD in vain.
3. You shall keep the Sabbath Day holy.
4. Honour your father and mother.
5. You shall not kill.
6. You shall not commit adultery.
7. You shall not steal.
8. You shall not bear false witness.
9. You shall not covet your neighbour's wife.
10. You shall not covet your neighbour's goods.

The Ten Commandments have a central place in teaching the faith, both ethically and theologically. Theologically they are superior to other laws in the Old Testament for by tradition they were written by the finger of God. Some have argued that the Decalogue is a type of contract between God and His people, based on agreements between vassal states and their overlords. These Commandments would be the terms of service for the people. The deal would have been ratified by Moses at the foot of Mount Sinai. The LORD would have assumed His duties to guard and guide the people with whom He was now in a formal relationship. This parallel has its uses but also its limitations. The People of God are not forced out of necessity or violence to take the LORD as their God, and the LORD's choice of the people of Israel is a preparation for the coming of Christ many centuries later. Vassal/overlord is not an adequate expression of the relationship between God and His chosen people.

    The laws of the rest of the *Torah* in many ways may be viewed as unpacking the fundamental principles of the Ten Commandments; what they say in principle the other laws say in detail. The law exists within the covenantal relationship. It is not a matter of keeping commandments and thus being the People of God. The relationship is the other way round. One is in a covenantal relationship with God and so one keeps the Ten Commandments. They are an expansion of what it means to be chosen and honoured by God from among the nations. As such they are not arbitrary laws but reflect the kind of people that the LORD wants to have as His own.

    What then do these Commandments enjoin on the people?

Traditionally the Commandments are said to operate in two directions: obligations to God and obligations to the community. This is an easy and logical division.

The first three concern obligations to God. They are based on the LORD who acts in history to save His people, and they are resolutely monotheistic: there is one God and one alone. We have seen in other passages in the Old Testament that such monotheism seems to develop in relatively late theology. In the Ten Commandments monotheism is justified solidly by the foundational rules which govern the people, and which in turn are based on the revelation of God. We know that the prohibitions on serving other gods and worshipping images of them (by which is meant the gods of the nations) were frequently broken by the people in subsequent generations. This was the main reason for the destruction of the Kingdoms in the lead up to the Babylonian Exile. The people did not do that which the LORD had commanded them, and so they were punished. The commandment not to take the name of the LORD in vain has been mentioned above. Keeping the Sabbath holy was both a reflection of the actions of God in the creation of the world as recorded in the first creation account, and also an observable, defining feature of the Jews as a nation and as a race. We have seen how this was to become increasingly important in the testing times of the Exile.

After these obligations to God come the obligations which bind the people together as a community. These are the rules which would govern any society of peoples. They are not specifically "Israelite" or "Jewish". Here a modern mind may well say that this proves that societal law is not dependent upon God; any society needs the same kinds of laws and they do not need to come from God. It is, however, equally valid to say that as all basic rules of society are the same, they come from one source; the source who created and guides the fortunes of all peoples through time and space. Commandments three to ten deal with this area. Murder and lying must be condemned (Commandments five and eight) and no group of people can function well over any prolonged period of time unless there is protection of property. The prohibitions against adultery and theft (six and seven) cover this.

The last two which concern coveting are more Commandments of the heart rather than having any practical application. It would be difficult to prove in a court of law that a man had been coveting his neighbour's goat! If anything this is a kind of moral law. It describes the stage before a culpable action. The only Commandment which has not yet been dealt with is the fourth, the command to honour father and mother. This is a societal command as it cements the family bonds. The family is the basic unit of life as God has designed it to be lived.

We should not think of law as a burden laid on the hearts and minds of the people of Israel. Law is the outward expression of the relationship between God and His people, and, much more intimately, God and the individual heart. Law exists within the covenants of God to guide and rule His people so that they may grow and develop into the people that they are destined to be.

Law, prophets, revelation and yearning come together into a greater whole which is the desire of the soul for intimacy with its Creator.

12

PSALMS AND WORSHIP

So far we have looked at the Old Testament as a document in history which was formed by the Holy Spirit through a distinct process governed by geography, history and politics, as well as religion. If this is all the Old Testament is, however, then it is a dusty and dry work. We can never forget that this was, and indeed remains, a vibrant and lived religion. All religions need their rites and rituals and the Old Testament is no different. In this section of Psalms and Worship, we will look at the Book of Psalms and then at the main feasts and festivals of ancient Judaism.

The Book of Psalms has been described as the 'Hymn Book of the Second Temple'. This reminds us that Psalms are predominantly songs to be sung, and that they find their meaning in the worship of God. We do well to remember that these Psalms were not just for the period after the Exile; some of them would have been sung and prayed at the time of David and Solomon. Indeed, Psalms were not even limited to the time of the Temple worship; they were for any gathering where the praise of God took place.

The numbering of the Psalms can cause some confusion. There is a Hebrew numbering system and a Greek system. The Hebrew follows the Masoretic text, the Greek follows the Septuagint. In Catholic worship we use the Greek numbering, although it must be said that some modern Catholic works have started to favour the Hebrew numbering. In this work we will use the Catholic (thus the Greek) system. If you are looking up references in most non-Catholic Bibles, the Psalm number will be different in most cases. The differences are as follows:

Hebrew	Greek
1-8	
9-10	9
11-113	10-112
114-115	113
116	114-115
117-146	116-145
147	146-147
148-150	

The Book of Psalms is divided into five sections. This probably mirrors the division of the *Torah* (the law) into the five Books of Moses. The divisions are these: Psalms 1-40; Psalms 41-71; Psalms 72-88; Psalms 89-105, and Psalms 106-150. Each of the first four divisions ends with a similar phrase, "Blessed be the

LORD, the God of Israel, from everlasting to everlasting! Amen and Amen." This may be a later editorial technique for concluding the five sections of Psalms. There have been various attempts to impose further order in the Book of Psalms, but there is no strict movement within each Book. It is true that the 'feel' of the Psalms moves from Lament to Praise, but this is not always the case. There were earlier collections of Psalms other than the Book which we now possess, so it is not surprising that the end of the second Book of the Psalms (71:19-20) finishes not only with the formulaic ending, but also an additional note:

> Blessed be his glorious name for ever;
> may his glory fill the whole earth!
> Amen and Amen!
> The prayers of David, the son of Jesse, are ended.
> Psalm 71:19-20

Of course there are other Psalms ascribed to King David in the Psalter, but it seems that a collection of pre-existing songs, later merged into the Book of Psalms, ended at this point.

Who wrote the Psalms?

According to tradition, and also the headings of the Psalms, many of them were ascribed to King David. Approximately half of the Psalter is given over to David's composition. Some of these may well date from the time of King David and even from his own hand. After all we know that he was skilled on the harp, soothing the worries of King Saul so he must have possessed some musical ability. Specific Psalms are fixed by their titles to the

King at a definite point in history. An example of this is Psalm 50, the title of which reads:

> A Psalm of David, when Nathan the prophet came
> to him, after he had gone in to Bathsheba.
> Psalm 50.0

Perhaps this Psalm came from this specific time, but then again the meaning of the Psalm is quite general. As we saw with Wisdom literature being ascribed to King Solomon to give it authenticity, so the same process may have happened with the Psalms and their Davidic authorship. It is interesting to note that in the Septuagint as opposed to the Hebrew text, the number of Psalms which are ascribed to King David's authorship rises from 73 to 84.

Psalms were also written by the sons of Korah. In the Book of Numbers, Korah had rebelled against the establishment of Aaron and his line as priests of the LORD. Korah had incited 250 companions to complain to Moses. Moses commanded that they come before the LORD at the Tent of Meeting to see God's judgement on the situation. The LORD did not approve of Korah's rebellion and struck them all with fire. Korah's descendants were demoted to be singers in the Temple (according to the lists in I Chronicles 6) and also door keepers (I Chronicles 9). Their Psalms are 41-48, 83-84 and 86-87. They are focused on the Temple in Jerusalem and are assumed to be pre-Exilic. Only in such a setting could phrases like these be used:

The Old Testament

> Great is the LORD and greatly to be praised in the city of our God!
> His holy mountain, beautiful in elevation, is the joy of all the earth,
> Mount Zion, in the far north, the city of the great King.
> Within her citadels God has shown Himself a sure defence.
> For lo, the Kings assembled, they came on together.
> As soon as they saw it, they were astounded, they were in panic, they took to flight;
> trembling took hold of them there, anguish as of a woman in travail.
>
> Psalm 47:1-6

After the Exile, such language concerning the city of David is simply impossible except in apocalyptic terms.

Psalm 49 and 72-82 were composed by Asaph. Although Asaph as a historical figure is contemporary with King David, the Psalms ascribed to him speak of the destruction of the Temple in Jerusalem:

> Direct thy steps to the perpetual ruins; the enemy has destroyed everything in the sanctuary!
>
> Psalm 73:3

It is difficult to place these Psalms. The imagery is of divine judgement and they speak of God as a shepherd. Apart from this there are no positive clues for placing them at any particular time or in any specific setting.

Some Psalms are ascribed to individuals: Psalm 88 to Ethan the Ezrahite; Psalm 87 to Heman the Ezrahite; Psalms 38,

61 and 76 by Jeduthun and Psalm 89 to Moses himself. The rest of the Psalter is the work of King Solomon (Psalm 71-126).

Although the Psalms are attributed to these individuals, personal composition is hard to prove. In some cases, according to the content of the Psalm itself, it is unlikely. The Psalms, however, are concerned with many themes and worries, as well as rites and worship. Authorship is not of primary importance.

An important thing about Psalms is that they are supposed to be sung. Some are in strange grammatical forms, an example of which we will see below, but as a general rule, the Psalms are designed to be chanted or to be accompanied by music. Indeed the term for Psalm in Greek, ψαλμος, means a song that is accompanied on an instrument. Within the Psalms themselves various musical instruments are mentioned. There is a lyre in Psalm 32:2 "Praise the LORD with the lyre, make melody to him with the harp of ten strings!", and a harp in Psalm 56:8 "Awake, my soul! Awake, O harp and lyre! I will awake the dawn!" There are not just stringed instruments but also a trumpet and a horn in Psalm 97:6 "With trumpets and the sound of the horn make a joyful noise before the King, the LORD!" and a pipe in Psalm 150:4 "Praise him with timbrel and dance; praise him with strings and pipe!". The latter quotation leads us to the realm of percussion, with cymbals, hand drums and tambourines, such as Psalm 149:3 (as well as Psalm 150 just quoted) "Let them praise his name with dancing, making melody to him with timbrel and lyre!"

The Old Testament

Although there are references to musical instruments, we do not know what the psalms sounded like. There is no record of written music in the Old Testament and very little in the Ancient Near East as a whole. An exception to this is an ancient hymn in the Hurrian language which was discovered from the Canaanite city of Ugarit. What makes it remarkable is that it contains both the text and musical notation for a hymn. It dates from about 1200BC and is dedicated to the moon goddess Nikkal. Unfortunately the clay tablet is damaged to some extent. We cannot know what relationship this may have had to the singing of the psalms in ancient Israel, but it does give us a glimpse into the world of religious music.

In the Psalms there is an indication of some form of music, such as the line "according to the lilies" which appears in the title of Psalms 44 and 68. This may be a hymn tune. Another word which may indicate musical notation is *selah* which occurs in many of the psalms. We do not know what this word means. It may mean that something is to be played louder or softer. Some have suggested that it is a direction for people to stand or sit. In the Septuagint it is translated into Greek as *diapsalma* which means something like 'a musical interlude'. *Selah* often comes at the natural point of division in a Psalm. The form of a psalm may also give some indication of the way in which it would be recited. Here we think of Psalm 135:

>…the sun to rule over the day, for His steadfast love endures for ever;

> the moon and stars to rule over the night, for His steadfast love endures for ever;
> to Him who smote the first-born of Egypt, for His steadfast love endures for ever;
> and brought Israel out from among them, for His steadfast love endures for ever;
> with a strong hand and an outstretched arm, for His steadfast love endures for ever;
> to Him who divided the Red Sea in sunder, for His steadfast love endures for ever…
>
> Psalm 135:8-13

This is just one section of the Psalm which rehearses the whole of the creative work of God, both in nature and in history. God creates the moon and stars as well as bringing His people up from the land of Egypt. Here, however, we want to consider the refrain, 'for his steadfast love endures forever'. Liturgically, or ritually, this lends itself to recitation between a cantor and the people. The cantor would lead the reading or singing of the first part and the people would sing the response. This happens today in the recitation of litanies of the Saints. The names of Saints are sung by a cantor, and the people respond 'pray for us'. This explains their repetitive style.

It is notoriously difficult to categorise the Psalms. All we can do here is to point out some of the main types and describe them.

The majority of the Psalms are Lament Psalms. They either concern an individual person or are a common lament of the nation. These usually begin with an appeal to God: 'I cry aloud to God, aloud to God, that he may hear me' (Psalm 76:1), and perhaps give a reason why the Psalmist is in this terrible position:

'For insolent men have risen against me, ruthless men seek my life; they do not set God before them' (Psalm 53:3). Sometimes the Psalmist stresses his innocence or confesses his guilt; 'For I know my transgressions, and my sin is ever before me' (Psalm 50.3). An appeal to the LORD is made and sometimes deliverance given: 'But I have trusted in thy steadfast love; my heart shall rejoice in thy salvation. I will sing to the LORD, because he has dealt bountifully with me' (Psalm 12: 5-6).

If this is the basic structure of the Psalms of Lament, what is their purpose? It is difficult to say who wrote them and to what end. It has been suggested that they were *pro forma* Psalms, so that if an individual came to the Temple for whatever reason, they could go to a Psalmist and ask him to sing a lament about a personal situation which had come about because of the malign influence of an 'enemy'. Perhaps a group of people were threatened by others, in which case Lament Psalms could also be sung/offered to God. This may seem a little strained, but in modern practice we have votive Masses which are used on various occasions and for various purposes, such as 'against enemies' or 'for a happy death' etc. It seems unlikely that individual Israelites went up to the Temple with their own hand-written offerings. The language is too exact and developed.

Some of the Lament Psalms are very specific, concerning illness. Illness and enemies are often mixed together. It is as if the wicked influence of those who decry an individual also brings about a physical effect in the body. We see this elsewhere in the

Old Testament, such as in the Wisdom literature in the Book of Job, where his illness is thought to be a result of his sin.

Spiritually, these Psalms of Lament are the most beautiful and haunting in the whole Psalter, for they speak of the human heart in everyday life, seeking and searching for God.

The second main type of Psalms are Psalms of Thanksgiving. A good example of this type is the shortest Psalm:

> Praise the LORD, all nations!
> Extol him, all peoples!
> For great is his steadfast love toward us;
> and the faithfulness of the LORD endures for ever.
> Praise the LORD!
>
> Psalm 116

This may be expanded to include various themes, for example Psalms 103 and 28 concern the creation of the whole world. Others praise the figure of Jerusalem, Mount Zion, such as Psalms 45, 47, 75, 83, 86 and 121.

If we follow the example given above, then the Thanksgiving Psalm would be the natural conclusion to a successful petition offered to God through a Lament Psalm. If a Communal Lament could be part of the nation's ritual response to God, so Communal Praise could remind God of His duty and relationship to His people. This grew in importance at the time of the deliverance from the Babylonian Exile.

Harpist playing and singing before the god Ra Harakhte.
XXI Dynasty, 1069-945 BC, Third Intermediate Period.
Stela. Louvre Museum, Paris.

As there are no easy divisions within the Psalms, so there are no overarching 'types' which encompass them all. We see historical Psalms, such as Psalm 135 mentioned above. Psalms can also be concerned with the big question of life, questions which are dealt with through wisdom literature, for example the first Psalm in the Psalter:

> Blessed is the man
> who walks not in the counsel of the wicked,
> nor stands in the way of sinners,
> nor sits in the seat of scoffers;
> but His delight is in the law of the LORD,
> and on His law he meditates day and night.
>
> Psalm 1:1-2

Other Psalms stress the centrality of following the law to bring happiness and salvation. An example is the longest Psalm, 118. This Psalm is also an acrostic. The letters which begin the lines of the Psalm, in sections of eight, follow the Hebrew alphabet: the first eight lines begin with the first letter, the second eight with the second and so on, making 176 verses, as there are 22 letters in the Hebrew alphabet. This is almost a school boy's exercise as well as a meditation on wisdom and suffering and the centrality of the law.

Other Psalms seem to need a ritual setting, for example Psalms 119-134, known as the Psalms of Ascent, when individuals 'go up' to Jerusalem. Others mention movement and processions:

> Walk about Zion, go round about her,
> number her towers,

consider well her ramparts,
go through her citadels…

Psalm 47:12

Others are concerned with entrance into the Temple:

Who shall ascend the hill of the LORD?
And who shall stand in His holy place?
He who has clean hands and a pure heart,
who does not lift up his soul to what is false,
and does not swear deceitfully…
Lift up your heads, O gates!
and be lifted up, O ancient doors!
that the King of glory may come in.

Psalm 23:3-7

Of course, as we have seen with much of the material in the Old Testament, it is easy to construct situations in which they can be used, but it is nigh on impossible to prove that was their setting or purpose.

Feasts

From the Psalms, let us turn to the feasts of the Old Testament. We will limit ourselves to the main feasts in Old Testament worship. We can only look at the 'official' religious practice. We do not know what happened in the countryside or during the reigns of the heretical Kings. Syncretism occurred, but this was never part of the true worship of the LORD.

This is not the place to develop a detailed explanation of the sacrifices and rites in Temple worship. That would be too lengthy and complicated. We will consider four festivals: Hanukkah, Tabernacles, Pentecost and Passover. The latter three were known as pilgrim feasts as they involved going up to the Temple or to a local sanctuary.

Hanukkah is the Festival of Lights and concerns the re-dedication of the Temple in Jerusalem after the Maccabean revolt in the second century BC. Jewish tradition tells of a miracle at the time of the re-dedication. The rite was to take eight days and a light needed to burn continuously. There was, however, only enough oil for one night. This was lit and miraculously lasted for all eight nights. This tradition is not found in the account in the First Book of Maccabees, which only speaks of eight days of celebration. This feast is included here, even though it touches only the fringe of the time of the Old Testament, because it shows that the religion of ancient Israel was dynamic. It did not end with the events long ago.

We turn now, however, to feasts which are associated with those ancient times.

The Feast of Tabernacles is variously called the Feast of Booths or of Ingathering. In Hebrew it is called *Sukkoth*. It is linked both to the religious history of God's salvation of His people as well as agricultural practices. It is also called the Feast of the Seventh Month. The three feasts together are described in the Book of Exodus as follows:

> Three times in the year you shall keep a feast to Me. You shall keep the feast of unleavened bread; as I commanded you, you shall eat unleavened bread for

seven days at the appointed time in the month of Abib, for in it you came out of Egypt. None shall appear before Me empty-handed. You shall keep the feast of harvest, of the first fruits of your labour, of what you sow in the field. You shall keep the feast of ingathering at the end of the year, when you gather in from the field the fruit of your labour. Three times in the year shall all your males appear before the Lord GOD.

Exodus 23:14-17

The Feast of Tabernacles is a feast of thanksgiving at the end of the harvest, giving thanks to God for the bounty of the land. It is agricultural in meaning and in religious practice. It is particularly associated with the fruit or grape harvest. In the history of the People of God it gained importance because it was the feast that was celebrated at significant times in their history. The Feast of Tabernacles was the first to be celebrated when the Exiles returned to the land. King Solomon had also dedicated the first Temple on the Feast of Tabernacles in I Kings 8. More than this Moses himself had associated this feast with the law:

> And Moses commanded them, "At the end of every seven years, at the set time of the year of release, at the feast of booths, when all Israel comes to appear before the LORD your God at the place which He will choose, you shall read this law before all Israel in their hearing.

Deuteronomy 31:10-11

Psalms and Worship

"The Jews' Passover" - *facsimile of a miniature from a 15th century Missal, ornamented with paintings of the School of Van Eyck.*

Even though the feast had been of great importance, the instructions recorded in Nehemiah seem to indicate that the specific details of the feast had been forgotten as time had passed:

> And they found it written in the law that the LORD had commanded by Moses that the people of Israel should dwell in booths during the feast of the seventh month, and that they should publish and proclaim in all their towns and in Jerusalem, "Go out to the hills and bring branches of olive, wild olive, myrtle, palm, and other leafy trees to make booths, as it is written."... And all the assembly of those who had returned from the captivity made booths and dwelt in the booths; for from the days of Jeshua the son of Nun to that day the people of Israel had not done so. And there was very great rejoicing. And day by day, from the first day to the last day, he read from the book of the law of God.
>
> Nehemiah 8:14-15, 17

The Book of Leviticus (chapter 23) tells us that the reason the people must dwell in booths. When they fled from Egypt the People of God dwelt in the very same type of booths as they made their way through the wilderness. However, the Old Testament is not consistent when describing the dwelling places of the Israelites as they journeyed through the wilderness. In the Book of Numbers, it states that they dwelt in tents, not booths. Tents seem more fitting to a nomadic existence. Such a way of life is in accord with wandering through the desert for forty years. The nature of booths indicates a more settled agricultural lifestyle. This would be more suitable at the time of the settlement in the land after the wilderness. This is reinforced by references which link the Feast of

Tabernacles with the end of year agricultural rites of thanksgiving; images much more at home in a vineyard than a desert.

It may be that a later Jewish festival, concerned with thanking God for the harvest, was 'historicised' (given a historical basis) in God's great works of salvation. The Feast of Tabernacles was transported back in time and attached to the period when the people were brought forth from the land of Egypt.

The next feast to consider is Pentecost. The term is Greek, meaning 'fifty days', πεντηκοστη, because this feast was kept fifty days after the offering of the barley sheaf during the Feast of Passover. It is also called the Feast of Weeks, the Feast of Reaping or First Fruits. In Hebrew it is called *Shavuot*. On the Passover a count began every day just before evening which was concluded on the fiftieth day.

Agriculturally the feast was connected to the grain harvest. This lasted seven weeks (fifty days) and was a time of rejoicing:

> You shall count seven weeks; begin to count the seven weeks from the time you first put the sickle to the standing grain. Then you shall keep the feast of weeks to the LORD your God with the tribute of a freewill offering from your hand, which you shall give as the LORD your God blesses you; and you shall rejoice before the LORD your God, you and your son and your daughter, your manservant and your maidservant, the Levite who is within your towns, the sojourner, the fatherless, and the widow who are among you, at the place which the LORD your God will choose, to make His name dwell there.
>
> Deuteronomy 16:9-11

Fifty days after the Passover was the first day on which this offering could be made to God. It also had a practical implication for it meant that the workers had to bring in the harvest for seven weeks before there could be rejoicing and celebration. First they must do the work, and only afterwards may they relax!

As we saw with the Feast of Tabernacles, this feast is also connected with the salvation of the People of God. In the narrative of bringing the people from Egypt, the Feast of *Shavuot* occurs fifty days after entering the wilderness and commemorates the moment when God gave the Ten Commandments to Moses on Mount Sinai. Every year the people had to count and wait in joyful anticipation for the covenantal agreement between God and His people. The Feast of Weeks/Pentecost is the culmination of this time of preparation and waiting.

There seems to have been a coalescing of an agricultural festival (the time needed for the corn harvest) and a historical moment when the law was given.

The final feast that we will consider is the greatest feast of all: the Passover.

Historically the Passover commemorates the last of the great plagues that the LORD sent upon the Pharaoh. All of the male firstborn Egyptians were killed, while the Jewish boys were spared. The LORD knew which houses to 'pass over' by the sign of blood which had been smeared on the lintel. When translated into Greek the term for this action was 'passing over', παρελευσεται. The name 'Passover' came from this term.

> Then Moses called all the elders of Israel, and said to them, "Select lambs for yourselves according to your families, and kill the passover lamb.
> Take a bunch of hyssop and dip it in the blood which is in the basin, and touch the lintel and the two doorposts with the blood which is in the basin; and none of you shall go out of the door of his house until the morning. For the LORD will pass through to slay the Egyptians; and when He sees the blood on the lintel and on the two doorposts, the LORD will pass over the door, and will not allow the destroyer to enter your houses to slay you. You shall observe this rite as an ordinance for you and for your sons for ever. And when you come to the land which the LORD will give you, as He has promised, you shall keep this service."
>
> Exodus 12:21-25

Apart from the 'passover lamb' being called the 'passover lamb' before the 'passover' has happened, this Festival makes sense. It connects history, linguistics, blood manipulation and the saving acts of God. When this is compared with the other rites surrounding the Festival then all falls into place. The bread had to remain unleavened because the Israelites did not have time for the leaven to rise before they had to flee Egypt. In the Books of Leviticus and Numbers the feast is also called the 'Feast of Unleavened Bread'. Unlike the Feast of Pentecost and the Feast of Tabernacles, Passover does not have agricultural symbolism at its centre. Baking unleavened bread and slaughtering lambs is entirely in keeping with a nomadic existence in the wilderness.

Passover was one of the great acts of the LORD. The other plagues had led Pharaoh to the point of freeing the Israelites, but it was the passing over of the avenging angel that proved to be decisive. Only after this could the people be led through the Red Sea and be given the Law on Mount Sinai, and only after this could the strength and the power of the LORD prove to the people that He was indeed their God.

The Passover has an ultimate significance in its fulfilment in Christ, which we shall look at below.

The religion of the Israelites is complex and involved. Much of it is not known. How the common people worshipped their God and lived their day-to-day lives will always remain shut off from us. We know of the round of sacrifices and offerings in the Temple, but as time passed, they changed.

Through all this uncertainty, however, one thing shines through; the Israelites worshipped the LORD who had saved them. Through their rites and rituals this was reinforced and made relevant in their changing circumstances. God had acted and continued to act to guard and guide His people until the moment of their justification.

It is to that justification that we now turn.

*The Prophet Daniel by Gianlorenzo Bernini in the Chigi Chapel of the Church of Santa Maria del Populo in Rome.
(1655-1661)*

13

APOCALYPSE AND THE COMING OF CHRIST

The term 'Apocalyptic' comes from Greek αποκαλυψις, *apokalupsis,* meaning to 'reveal' or 'unveil'. We saw in the early prophetic work that the future was revealed to prophets through dreams, visions, cleromancy and other means. God frequently manifested His will to His prophets in such ways. A vision had not only to be given, it must also be understood. This definition of Apocalyptic will serve us well. It is something which is given by the LORD, is connected with prophecy, and reveals His will for the future. The future intended, however, is not immediate. It concerns the culmination of time, the end of the age.

All through this work we have seen elements of Apocalyptic. One part of Apocalyptic is associated with the collapse of the Kingdoms and the reinterpretation of the Davidic covenant. Another comes from the aftermath of the Exile and is centred on the prophets. A third may be placed in the time of the settled religious existence after the Exile when Apocalyptic was a tool to be used for a secondary purpose.

As the people tried to understand their history, they focused on the person of King David. This was not for any historical reason; David was not an exemplary King when it came to the worship of the LORD. It was David, however, who had conquered Jerusalem. Though he had not built it, the Temple had become the place of the very presence of God on earth. The prophecies concerning David had extended his line, his descendants, to a non-specific future. II Samuel 7:16 declares:

> And your house and your Kingdom shall be made sure for ever before Me; your throne shall be established for ever.

By the time of his grandchildren, the one throne of King David had been divided. How could the throne be established forever, if it had already changed? Within a few hundred years, it had ceased to exist altogether! The only way of understanding the prophecy was that there would have to be a restoration of some kind of Kingship. The one who occupied this position would be a descendant of the great King David. As time passed the likelihood of its being a historical Kingdom with a historical King became more and more remote. The People, after the Exile, achieved a certain level of autonomy, but they never had a political system which wielded the power of the pre-Exilic Kingdoms. When client Kings were set up under foreign powers they would never claim to be the 'descendants of King David'. By this time, in the later period, the term had become overlaid with Messianic meaning and Apocalyptic overtones.

Who was the Messiah?

The term 'Messiah' referred to the ritual action of anointing. This was connected with Kingship in the early literature of the Old Testament, such as the anointing of Kings:

> Then Samuel took a vial of oil and poured it on his [Saul's] head, and kissed him and said, "Has not the LORD anointed you to be prince over his people Israel? And you shall reign over the people of the LORD and you will save them from the hand of their enemies round about. And this shall be the sign to you that the LORD has anointed you to be prince over his heritage."
>
> I Samuel 10:1

Anointing was not just reserved for Kings or, as we have seen in the section just quoted, for King David. Objects were anointed when they were set apart for sacred use such as the Temple utensils in Exodus 40. Even the foreign King, Cyrus, could be set apart for the greater plan of God:

> Thus says the LORD to his anointed, to Cyrus…
>
> Isaiah 45:1

The term 'Messiah' developed over time, and we should expect this in Apocalyptic Literature. As the Scribes pored over the holy texts they would have found terms and prophecies which had not been fulfilled and they would have tried to understand why such prophecies had been given to the people in the first place. The answer was found in the future, in the Apocalypse. Even before

King David, prophecies abounded such as the words of Jacob to his son Judah:

> The sceptre shall not depart from Judah, nor the ruler's staff from between his feet, until he comes to whom it belongs; and to him shall be the obedience of the peoples.
>
> Genesis 49:10

We do not know whether or not this is a *bona fide* prophetic Apocalyptic utterance, but there is enough material to weave together a yearning for a future leader who would fulfil the destiny of the great Kings.

The Psalms were rich mines for such Apocalyptic images. Psalm 71 declared the coming Messiah would have boundless power and the obedience of all the nations:

> May He have dominion from sea to sea, and from the River to the ends of the earth!
> May His foes bow down before Him, and His enemies lick the dust!
> May the Kings of Tarshish and of the isles render Him tribute, may the Kings of Sheba and Seba bring gifts!
> May all Kings fall down before Him, all nations serve Him!
>
> Psalm 71:8-11

There are at least two threads of Messianic hope intertwined in the images in the Old Testament. There was a belief that the Messiah would come and would restore the fortunes of Israel. This, naturally, would be at the expense of the surrounding countries. At the same time there was an expansion of the Apocalyptic vision of the Messiah. This did not lead to the destruction of the other peoples but rather incorporated them. Such was the case when Cyrus, the foreigner, was called a 'Messiah'. He should not be confused with an Apocalyptic Messianic figure, but it shows that the LORD's salvific will was not limited to His chosen people.

At this time we would expect a break with the historical figure of David, however, the opposite happens. The Book of Ezekiel explicitly links the Messiah with King David:

> And I will set up over them one shepherd, My servant David, and he shall feed them: he shall feed them and be their shepherd. And I, the LORD, will be their God, and My servant David shall be prince among them; I, the LORD, have spoken.
>
> Ezekiel 34:23-24

It is not clear whether this calls for a leader 'like' David of old, or whether the Messiah is to be some from of Davidic, anointed, semi-mythical individual.

At the time of the Exile there was another development in the Messianic vision within the Old Testament. Whereas for some the Messiah was to be the great military figure, for others this type of hero was no longer relevant. This change is found in the famous Servant Songs of the second part of the Book of the Prophet Isaiah. We cannot know how important these songs were to the contemporary mind, but they have a great significance in the later identification of the Messiah with the figure of Christ. The Servant Songs appear in Isaiah 42:1-7; 49:1-6; 50:4-9 and 52:13-

53:12. The extraordinary thing about the man portrayed in then is that he went against the prevalent wisdom of the time. To lead a nation one must be strong. To vindicate a people one must be victorious. The Servant does not have these attributes. The mission of the Servant is not only to the People of God but also to the nations. The nations were not going to be destroyed or brought low, rather the Servant was to bring 'light' to the Gentiles:

> Behold My servant, whom I uphold, My chosen, in whom My soul delights; I have put My Spirit upon him, he will bring forth justice to the nations... I am the LORD, I have called you in righteousness, I have taken you by the hand and kept you; I have given you as a covenant to the people, a light to the nations, to open the eyes that are blind, to bring out the prisoners from the dungeon, from the prison those who sit in darkness.
>
> Isaiah 42:1, 6-7

There is a universality in the role of the Servant, which we will encounter again as we look at other types of Apocalyptic literature. The way the Servant was to bring this about is quite startling. It is not through the manifestation of might, but rather through suffering. There is transference of punishment from the People of God to the Servant. This is why he is called the 'suffering Servant'. Through punishing him, the LORD can repeal the punishment due to the nation. By his wounds Israel is redeemed. These are the most beautiful and poetic passages in the whole of the Old Testament. The nature of leadership is redefined and God's relationship to His people is subtly changed:

> He was despised and rejected by men; a man of sorrows, and acquainted with grief; and as one from whom men hide their faces he was despised, and we esteemed him not.
> Surely he has borne our griefs and carried our sorrows; yet we esteemed him stricken, smitten by God, and afflicted.
> But he was wounded for our transgressions, he was bruised for our iniquities; upon him was the chastisement that made us whole, and with his stripes we are healed.
> All we like sheep have gone astray; we have turned every one to his own way; and the LORD has laid on him the iniquity of us all.
>
> Isaiah 53:3-6

This was not the Messiah who had been expected.

We should not suppose that Apocalyptic developed in a linear manner. At various points in history, and indeed to various groups within the Old Testament time frame, different thoughts and ideas occurred at different moments. When Kingdoms still existed, the People of God could hope for an Israelite (or more correctly Judahite) King who would come and slaughter the enemies of the people and restore the land, possessions and status of the nation. The Messiah would be a military leader, strong in power and mighty in battle. As the Kingdoms and the land were taken by aggressors this Davidic King became a Messianic figure who would be the one who would restore the people to the land. Cyrus fitted the description well. After the Exile, the Davidic Messiah would be neither a King, nor a military figure; he had become something else. Even the great Mattathias at the time of the Maccabean revolt was not the Messiah. In part, the Book of

Jubilees, which is not a canonical work and so is not included in the Bible, tried to address the issue of the Davidic Messiah and the Maccabean revolt. In it, the age of the Maccabees is counted as the beginning of the Messianic age, and the promises made to Levi are portrayed as more important than those made to Judah. Why was this done? The Maccabean victors were descendants of the tribe of Levi, while the Messianic promises were made to the Tribe of Judah. It was sufficiently important for the author of Jubilees that the saviour of the people had to come from the Davidic line that he made a justification of the role of the Maccabees in his Book. He merged Levi with Judah, so that the prophecies would stand.

As time passed, the new, real, Messiah was pushed into the future. He would appear at the end of time, in Greek the *eschaton*.

As we looked at the canonical work of the prophets we saw that they each had different concerns. Some brought condemnation on current social, religious or moral practice. Others prophesied about the consequences of the decisions of the nations and peoples. Some gave comfort in trouble and others advice in restoration. After the Exile, the role and the character of the prophets changed. As the Exiles returned, their theology, under the influence of the Deuteronomists and the Priests, became much more focused on the correct interpretation and implementation of the law. It was by following the law that the land could be secure. The traditional position of the prophet had been marginalized. The scribes occupied the place of the court prophets and the observance of the law negated the need for social and moral prophetic utterances.

In the earlier prophetic works, judgement had always been an integral part of the message. In the early sections of the prophet Isaiah, the judgement would come on the people because they had not followed the ways of the LORD their God. Judgement in Amos was a real threat to the People of God. As the LORD had judged others, so He would judge Israel. In order to persuade people to change their ways there had to be a reason. This was the wrath of God. It was understood most fully not in personal judgement but in the national destruction which had been brought about on both Kingdoms at the hand of the LORD. These judgements were to happen on the 'Day of the LORD'. This 'Day' was described in many ways, and was surrounded by many images:

> "And on that day," says the Lord GOD, "I will make the sun go down at noon, and darken the earth in broad daylight."
>
> Amos 8:9

> ...you [Ariel] will be visited by the LORD of hosts with thunder and with earthquake and great noise, with whirlwind and tempest, and the flame of a devouring fire.
>
> Isaiah 29:6

Through this process of judgement in these early prophetic works, the nation would be judged, but it was always for their own good. It ended in their purity and the restoration of their relationship with God. This national vision become more and more restricted as the judgement was expanded. As the Day of the Lord began to include not just Israel but all nations it became a world judgement. It was no longer Israel against the world. Now it was the righteous of the nations, including Israel, who were to be judged. This judgement would not find the whole of the People of God faithful, but only a remnant within them. We see this in the Book of Zephaniah.

Zephaniah is a whirlwind of passion. The vision which he gave was one of unalloyed violence and justice. The LORD would judge everyone. The thrust of the prophecy was against the nations, but the People of God were not excluded. The prophets seemed to assume that not all of the people would be excluded from the wrath of God. There would be a faithful group which would remain loyal to the LORD and thus would be rewarded:

> The remnant of My people shall plunder them [the Moabites and Ammonites], and the survivors of My nation shall possess them.
>
> Zephaniah 2:9b

We can see how this process developed in the time of the Exile. Not all people had profaned the LORD's name, and so not all should be punished. The faithful few would be rewarded. Righteousness did not reside in one people, but in the action and beliefs of individuals within the nation. If nations as a whole were no longer held to be righteous or evil, then the judgement could no longer be painted with such large brush strokes. The universal judgement presupposes the universal nature of the reign of God.

The role of the Messiah had also expanded. The Apocalyptic vision included all peoples, nations and individuals. All would be called before the LORD. All nations must be converted to the LORD so the LORD would truly hold sway over the whole earth.

From this Apocalyptic vision comes a further stage; the incorporation of the nations into the worship of Almighty God. The prophet Zechariah described the terrible warfare and slaughter which would happen when nations and people opposed the LORD and his Holy City. Once the carnage has stopped, however, a new situation would come about:

> Then every one that survives of all the nations that have come against Jerusalem shall go up year after year to worship the King, the LORD of hosts, and to keep the feast of booths.
> And if any of the families of the earth do not go up to Jerusalem to worship the King, the LORD of hosts, there will be no rain upon them.
> And if the family of Egypt do not go up and present themselves, then upon them shall come the plague with which the LORD afflicts the nations that do not go up to keep the feast of booths.
> This shall be the punishment to Egypt and the punishment to all the nations that do not go up to keep the feast of booths.
>
> Zechariah 14:16-19

The language still seems to be about judgement and punishment, but what lies behind it is the incorporation of the nations into the public worship of God. Apocalyptic does not just denote universal judgement, it also offers universal salvation. The focus of salvation is the same, the indwelling presence of the LORD on His Holy Mountain, but the entry criteria have been radically changed:

> It shall come to pass in the latter days that the mountain of the house of the LORD shall be established as the highest of the mountains, and shall be raised up above the hills; and peoples shall flow to it, and many nations shall come, and say: "Come, let us go up to the mountain of the LORD, to the house of the God of Jacob; that He may teach us His ways and we may walk in His paths." For out of Zion shall go forth the law and the word of the LORD from Jerusalem."
>
> Micah 4:1-2

The way to salvation, following the law, was available to all peoples. The images surrounding this great moment are visions of plenty. We see it in the Book of the Prophet Amos:

> "Behold, the days are coming," says the LORD, "when the ploughman shall overtake the reaper and the treader of grapes him who sows the seed; the mountains shall drip sweet wine, and all the hills shall flow with it."
>
> Amos 9:13

This time will be a new creation, a new heaven and earth which will somehow restore the great days of former times. This hope in the end times was not uniform in the Old Testament. Indeed it only gained prominence in Jewish mysticism towards the time of Christ. The works produced then are beyond the scope of this work, as they do not fall into the canon of the Old Testament. We can, however, observe their trend. Some of these works believed that in the Messianic times there would be an exact and explicit reconstruction of the former days. The tribes would rise again, so that the Sons of Jacob could once more be constituted as the People of God. The dead would rise (and here we can see the great conflict which would grow between the Sadducees, who did not accept the resurrection of the dead, and the Pharisees, who did) and judgement would be made. The prophets Elijah, Moses and Enoch would come to earth and herald the Kingdom of the Messiah. The whole world would come to Jerusalem and worship God.

This, however, was in the future.

We turn to the last type of Apocalyptic that we wish to consider. We said above that this was where Apocalyptic was used to serve another purpose. Let us look at the prophet Daniel.

It is with some trepidation that we approach the Book of Daniel. Daniel is commonly called a Prophet, but the work is scarcely prophetic, and indeed the Hebrew canon includes it with the 'Writings' rather than the 'Prophets'. It claims to record history, but the imagery which it uses does not have the feel of other historical works in the Old Testament. We included it here in Apocalyptic because of the visions which occur and because of the phrase 'one like the son of man' (Daniel 7:13) which later gained such importance in Christian circles.

Let us put Daniel into some context. The work can be divided in two. First is the section which records Daniel's life (chapters 1-6), after which his prophecies occur (chapters 7-12). The Book includes a long, sustained section of Aramaic. There is no obvious reason for this, but there are many speculations. The dating of Daniel is controversial. The text itself is concerned with the time of the Exile and one could assume that it was written immediately after the return to the land. This, however, does not seem to be the case. The terms used for certain Kings, the identification of Daniel with Joseph and also the identification of the fourfold images with ages or eras, do not fit with an exact dating. Most scholars converge on the Book of Daniel being written in response to the persecution of Antiochus IV Epiphanes who ruled from 175-164BC. It may be that court stories and histories existed before concerning a figure called 'Daniel', and these were developed into the final form of the work. In the Book of Ezekiel, the name 'Daniel' belongs to a wise man (Ezekiel 14:14), so the Book may be referring to a person of wisdom in the past, rather than a specific individual. Also within the canon of the Old Testament there may be a further link between the Book of Daniel and the time of Antiochus. In I Maccabees 1:54, Antiochus "erected a desolating sacrilege upon the altar of burnt offering". This 'Abomination of Desolation' seems to be the same as that which is mentioned in Daniel 9:27 and 11:31.

If this is the case, the visions in the second part of Daniel's work gain special significance for they would have been written at a time of historical turmoil. They would be based in history and would comment upon it. We can see this clearly when the Angel Gabriel provides an interpretation for Daniel's vision of the beasts and the horns:

> He [Gabriel] said, "Behold, I will make known to you what shall be at the latter end of the indignation; for it pertains to the appointed time of the end. As for the ram which you saw with the two horns, these are the Kings of Media and Persia. And the he-goat is the King of Greece; and the great horn between his eyes is the first King. As for the horn that was broken, in place of which four others arose, four Kingdoms shall arise from his nation, but not with his power. And at the latter end of their rule, when the transgressors have reached their full measure, a King of bold countenance, one who understands riddles, shall arise. His power shall be great, and he shall cause fearful destruction, and shall succeed in what he does, and destroy mighty men and the people of the saints. By his cunning he shall make deceit prosper under his hand, and in his own mind he shall magnify himself. Without warning he shall destroy many; and he shall even rise up against the Prince of princes; but, by no human hand, he shall be broken. The vision of the evenings and the mornings which has been told is true; but seal up the vision, for it pertains to many days hence."
>
> Daniel 8:19-26

This text is quoted in full because the explanation for this vision is clear and exact. The other visions, however, are not explained. The famous vision of the statue made out of various forms of metal with feet of clay in chapter two is not clear, neither are the visions of the four beasts in chapter seven and of the battles between the King of the North and the King of the South in chapter eleven. The work falls into Apocalyptic more specifically because the last and greatest Kingdom in the visions will last for ever.

    The conundrum of interpretation is at the heart of the Book of Daniel and is central to its Apocalyptic nature. It is a riddle which needs a key to unlock it. As some of the visions are obviously and explicitly historical, one can assume that the other visions are similarly related to history. If we look at any series of commentaries on the Book of Daniel, then we will see that the interpretation of the visions is still open to much conjecture. This is not just from a faith perspective (the need to read into a text a specific interpretation) but also from a scholarly one. Daniel does not provide a key to his visions, except in the case quoted above. Some of them are clear, most are not. We simply need to acknowledge that there are historical figures behind the Apocalyptic language.

Apocalyptic literature provides a cover for subversive material to be disseminated. The faithful could read and understand the codes included in Daniel's visions and gain comfort from them. What they were describing would be obvious to the few, but opaque to the many. Open criticism of the political regime would have resulted in further oppression. This underground material provided a destabilising influence, while, on the surface level, remaining politically neutral.

The success of this Apocalyptic material is shown by the fact that they are still being interpreted. The visions are clear and strong and cry out for meaning. Even if the original context is gone, the visions remain.

For our purpose we have no need to try to decode the historical meanings of the Kingdoms. They point to a meaning which is beyond them and indeed to a meaning which was beyond the intention of their author.

We must look for a moment at the 'son of man' in Daniel's visions:

> I saw in the night visions, and behold, with the clouds of heaven there came one like a son of man, and he came to the Ancient of Days and was presented before him. And to him was given dominion and glory and Kingdom, that all peoples, nations, and languages should serve him; his dominion is an everlasting dominion, which shall not pass away, and his Kingdom one that shall not be destroyed.
>
> Daniel 7:13-14

To this we may add the vision of the one who was like a 'son of the gods' in the fiery furnace of chapter 3:25. In modern Old Testament interpretation, following Jewish practice, the term simply means 'a human being' as opposed to a divine being. If the phase is given any Messianic interpretation, then it comes to mean a semi-divine being such as the Archangel Michael. This may be a later down playing of the phrase. We know that much has been made by Christianity of this term, so it is not beyond the realms of possibility that its Messianic meaning within scholarship has been watered down in response to Christianity's elevation of it. The Ancient of Days is clearly a title of God, the LORD. The 'son of man', no matter who he is, is someone who is entrusted with the administration of the governance of the whole world on behalf of God. This Kingdom is everlasting. This is Messianic Apocalyptic material without doubt.

Here we move from the Apocalyptic to the coming of Christ.

The Coming of Christ

We can understand the Old Testament on many levels. We saw this at the beginning of this work when looking at 'Methods and Approaches of Interpretation'. We have concentrated on looking at the text of the Old Testament itself and at the surrounding countries to try to understand what it meant at various points though certain types of literature.

This final section of this book seems to jar with this manner of looking at our Sacred text. We jump from one way of considering the Scriptures to another. How can we look critically at the Old Testament and then seek to interpret it in the light of a revelation which seemingly comes from outside it? How can we try to understand the inner meaning and working of the history and theology of the Ancient Israelites, and then filter it all through the mesh of Christianity, and specifically Catholicism?

There is neither need nor space for a whole scale revision of what we have said above in the light of the revelation of Christ through our Mother the Church, but we do a disservice to our faith, and thus to the Old Testament if we ignore this essential element and purpose of these Scriptures.

When we began to define what Scripture was and what it contained at the very beginning of this work, we did so from an unashamedly Catholic standpoint. The Church defined the

The Old Testament

Scriptures and gave them authority. We can interpret them in a way which is not only consonant with the texts themselves but also with the deposit of faith found in the Church.

With this in mind, just for a moment, let us look at the coming of Christ in the pages of the Old Testament.

Books have been written which search out any trace or image which could point to the coming of Christ. They scoured the pages of the Old Testament to seek any reference made in the New Testament to the Old. This seems to be an honourable, if futile exercise. The disciples were Jews. Our Lady was a Jewess. Our Lord was steeped in the Scriptures. It would have been extraordinary if images, half remembered texts and allusions did not find their way onto the lips of all religious thinkers and teachers at the time of Our Lord.

Such typology is not our purpose here.

The core belief of Catholicism is the person and nature of Christ. We have seen in the Old Testament how the People of God had to be led and their faith developed to move from one stage to the next. We saw that monotheism was not integral at the beginning of the call of Abraham. We know that the primitive understanding of the nature of God had to give away to something that was greater, and one must say, more correct. The world of the gods, as a way of explaining the random elements of the universe, was not satisfactory for a developed religion, and did not portray the reality of the nature of God.

This is something which is vitally important. The way that the People of God understood the LORD was not their response to the situation which surrounded them. It may be fashionable to explain away religion by saying that it is the result of external pressures, but such a faith would and could never stand the test of time. The faith of the people of the Old Testament was guided in a certain way because it corresponded to the essence of God, and to the truth that He revealed to His creation. It was all about the way they should live, what they should do and how they were to worship, as well as showing something of the very nature of God Himself.

The development in understanding corresponded to the ability of the people to absorb and accept it. Monotheism only really had a meaning when the gods of the nations were powerless to derail the path and plan of the people whom God had chosen. Monotheism could not have been revealed in the very early period of Old Testament history. It would have been meaningless. Only as time passed could the people see that this was the only way to understand their God.

The nation also had to realise that they could not put their trust in Kings and political figures. They needed to reject the LORD's injunction that monarchy was not a system of governance for them, so that they could really understand the reign of God. They had trusted in their own power and might through their military and religious rulers. Again and again these had failed, eventually leading to the loss of the land which had been the physical sign of God's covenantal love. Only then did they realise their situation and remember that the LORD had said that He alone was to be their King. What did it mean that God was King? Well experience human Kingship and see its weaknesses and poverty, then know and appreciate God and His reign.

The Israelites were shown the nature of God through His steadfast love to them through all of the covenants and His dogged persistence in never letting go of the people whom He had chosen for His own. The final covenant, the covenant of love inscribed in their hearts, spoke of a tenderness and love between God and His people that cannot be paralleled. This is not some deity who wields a high hand, lays down the law and then curses or leaves His people at the first problem. Yes, the language speaks of judgement and punishment, but only as a parent who loves so much that they must teach their child by harsh lessons.

The nation had to be brought low so that it could fully appreciate what it was to be exalted high above the heavens. It must have its identity stripped so that the true nature of the role that it was to perform was clear and true. It could not think of itself in opposition to the other nations, for it was to incorporate all nations to itself. It was to show to all peoples that the LORD was judge of the whole world and this His love was universal.

The LORD formed His people not only through rules and regulations, a simple tit-for-tat faith based on mutual advancement, but rather through a law to be lived. This was no set of dry prescriptions. The law was yoked to the prophets so that the ethical and moral elements of a person's life were placed not in conflict with the law but as the perfection and fulfilment of it. The law was indeed to shine forth from Zion, for it was of God. It was to teach the people holiness and sanctity, right judgement and honest dealing. It was to be kept with all of the exhortations that the prophets could muster. An individual should not just obey, but obedience should become part of his very identity.

The prophets spoke of the will and desire of God. They announced His judgements and warned of His wrath, but they spoke also of His unutterable love and His suffering for His people. They spoke of the Messiah who was to come. They spoke of the culmination of all time.

The Psalms sang of the LORD. Wisdom plumbed the depths of the human dilemma.

All was in place. All was prepared.

The utterances and witness of the Old Testament in every letter and in every stroke of the pen spoke of the one who was to come. It was He who was to fulfil the prophecies, who was to be the reason for the law; He who was the end of history, to whom all development pointed. He was the Messiah, the anointed, the one who suffered out of love. It was He who broke the bonds of one God for only one nation and bound anew the whole world in His mercy.

The people of the Old Testament were His chosen race, chosen from the dawn of time to prepare the world for His coming. His covenant with them shines with the beauty and majesty of God.

The Old Testament

And Christ came and walked among us.

He is the Testament, both Old and New.

Amen, Amen.

14

Afterword

It can be daunting for people to approach the Old Testament. It is so full of strange names and people. It covers such a long time period that the temptation is simply to give up and leave it to the 'experts'.

I would like to thank the people of my parish of St George in Warminster for attending the course on the Old Testament, from which this book sprang. Fr Alexander Redman has reviewed the script and made many suggestions. Dr Francesca Stavrakopoulou was good enough to look through the manuscript; though I am sure that she will not agree with some of the theological sentiments expressed herein!

As a parish priest I am well aware that these Scriptures are proclaimed week after week in our Churches. The Old Testament is read as the 'Word of the Lord' but can be a closed book to the majority of people in the pews. I hope that this work will give people confidence to engage with the ancient writings of our faith.

We know and we believe that the world was prepared from countless generations for the coming of Christ. If we do not understand the way in which God moved through history, then we can never hope to see His actions in our present time. If we cannot see His guiding hand in the worship and theological understanding of His people, we will miss His message for today.

"In the beginning God created the Heavens and the Earth..."

May He who formed us in our mother's womb sanctify and guide us so that we may come to love and honour Him.

May our Holy Mother the Church preserve and guard the Scriptures entrusted to her care and may we all come one day to the joys of everlasting life.

Amen.

The Old Testament

Appendix A

The Council of Trent

April 8th, 1546
Session iv
Decree concerning the Sacred Scriptures

The sacred and holy, ecumenical, and general Synod of Trent, - lawfully assembled in the Holy Ghost, the Same three legates of the Apostolic See presiding therein, - keeping this always in view, that, errors being removed, the purity itself of the Gospel be preserved in the Church; which (Gospel), before promised through the prophets in the holy Scriptures, our Lord Jesus Christ, the Son of God, first promulgated with His own mouth, and then commanded to be preached by His Apostles to every creature, as the fountain of all, both saving truth, and moral discipline; and seeing clearly that this truth and discipline are contained in the written books, and the unwritten traditions which, received by the Apostles from the mouth of Christ Himself, or from the Apostles themselves, the Holy Ghost dictating, have come down even unto us, transmitted as it were from hand to hand; (the Synod) following the examples of the orthodox Fathers, receives and

Appendix A - The Council of Trent

venerates with an equal affection of piety, and reverence, all the books both of the Old and of the New Testament—seeing that one God is the author of both —as also the said traditions, as well those appertaining to faith as to morals, as having been dictated, either by Christ's own word of mouth, or by the Holy Ghost, and preserved in the Catholic Church by a continuous succession.

And it has thought it meet that a list of the sacred books be inserted in this decree, lest a doubt may arise in any one's mind, which are the books that are received by this Synod. They are as set down here below:

Of the Old Testament: the five books of Moses, to wit, Genesis, Exodus, Leviticus, Numbers, Deuteronomy; Josue, Judges, Ruth, four books of Kings, two of Paralipomenon, the first book of Esdras, and the second which is entitled Nehemias; Tobias, Judith, Esther, Job, the Davidical Psalter, consisting of a hundred and fifty psalms; the Proverbs, Ecclesiastes, the Canticle of Canticles, Wisdom, Ecclesiasticus, Isaias, Jeremias, with Baruch; Ezechiel, Daniel; the twelve minor prophets, to wit, Osee, Joel, Amos, Abdias, Jonas, Micheas, Nahum, Habacuc, Sophonias, Aggaeus, Zacharias, Malachias; two books of the Machabees, the first and the second.

Of the New Testament: the four Gospels, according to Matthew, Mark, Luke, and John; the Acts of the Apostles written by Luke the Evangelist; fourteen epistles of Paul the apostle, (one) to the Romans, two to the Corinthians, (one) to the Galatians, to the Ephesians, to the Philippians, to the Colossians, two to the Thessalonians, two to Timothy, (one) to Titus, to Philemon, to the

Hebrews; two of Peter the apostle, three of John the apostle, one of the apostle James, one of Jude the apostle, and the Apocalypse of John the apostle.

But if any one receive not, as sacred and canonical, the said books entire with all their parts, as they have been used to be read in the Catholic Church, and as they are contained in the old Latin vulgate edition; and knowingly and deliberately contemn the traditions aforesaid; let him be anathema. Let all, therefore, understand, in what order, and in what manner, the said Synod, after having laid the foundation of the Confession of faith, will proceed, and what testimonies and authorities it will mainly use in confirming dogmas, and in restoring morals in the Church.

Appendix B

Divino Afflante Spiritu

Encyclical of Pope Pius XII, 30th September 1943

10. But it is right and pleasing to confess openly that it is not only by reason of these initiatives, precepts and exhortations of Our Predecessors that the knowledge and use of the Sacred Scriptures have made great progress among Catholics; for this is also due to the works and labours of all those who diligently cooperated with them, both by meditating, investigating and writing, as well as by teaching and preaching and by translating and propagating the Sacred Books. For from the schools in which are fostered higher studies in theological and biblical science, and especially from Our Pontifical Biblical Institute, there have already come forth, and daily continue to come forth, many students of Holy Scripture who, inspired with an intense love for the Sacred Books, imbue the younger clergy with this same ardent zeal and assiduously impart to them the doctrine they themselves have acquired. Many of them also, by the written word, have promoted and do still promote, far and wide, the study of the Bible; as when they edit the sacred text corrected in accordance with the rules of

Appendix B – Divino Afflante Spiritu

textual criticism or expound, explain, and translate it into the vernacular; or when they propose it to the faithful for their pious reading and meditation; or finally when they cultivate and seek the aid of profane sciences which are useful for the interpretation of the Scriptures. From these therefore and from other initiatives which daily become more wide-spread and vigorous, as, for example, biblical societies, congresses, libraries, associations for meditation on the Gospels, We firmly hope that in the future reverence for, as well as the use and knowledge of, the Sacred Scriptures will everywhere more and more increase for the good of souls, provided the method of biblical studies laid down by Leo XIII, explained more clearly and perfectly by his Successors, and by Us confirmed and amplified - which indeed is the only safe way and proved by experience - be more firmly, eagerly and faithfully accepted by all, regardless of the difficulties which, as in all human affairs, so in this most excellent work will never be wanting.

11. There is no one who cannot easily perceive that the conditions of biblical studies and their subsidiary sciences have greatly changed within the last fifty years. For, apart from anything else, when Our Predecessor published the Encyclical Letter Providentissimus Deus, hardly a single place in Palestine had begun to be explored by means of relevant excavations. Now, however, this kind of investigation is much more frequent and, since more precise methods and technical skill have been developed in the course of actual experience, it gives us information at once more abundant and more accurate. How much light has been derived from these explorations for the more

correct and fuller understanding of the Sacred Books all experts know, as well as all those who devote themselves to these studies. The value of these excavations is enhanced by the discovery from time to time of written documents, which help much towards the knowledge of the languages, letters, events, customs, and forms of worship of most ancient times. And of no less importance is papyri which have contributed so much to the knowledge of the discovery and investigation, so frequent in our times, of letters and institutions, both public and private, especially of the time of Our Saviour.

33. As in our age, indeed new questions and new difficulties are multiplied, so, by God's favour, new means and aids to exegesis are also provided. Among these it is worthy of special mention that Catholic theologians, following the teaching of the Holy Fathers and especially of the Angelic and Common Doctor, have examined and explained the nature and effects of biblical inspiration more exactly and more fully than was wont to be done in previous ages. For having begun by expounding minutely the principle that the inspired writer, in composing the sacred book, is the living and reasonable instrument of the Holy Spirit, they rightly observe that, impelled by the divine motion, he so uses his faculties and powers, that from the book composed by him all may easily infer "the special character of each one and, as it were, his personal traits." Let the interpreter then, with all care and without neglecting any light derived from recent research, endeavour to determine the peculiar character and circumstances of the sacred

writer, the age in which he lived, the sources written or oral to which he had recourse and the forms of expression he employed.

35. What is the literal sense of a passage is not always as obvious in the speeches and writings of the ancient authors of the East, as it is in the works of our own time. For what they wished to express is not to be determined by the rules of grammar and philology alone, nor solely by the context; the interpreter must, as it were, go back wholly in spirit to those remote centuries of the East and with the aid of history, archaeology, ethnology, and other sciences, accurately determine what modes of writing, so to speak, the authors of that ancient period would be likely to use, and in fact did use.

36. For the ancient peoples of the East, in order to express their ideas, did not always employ those forms or kinds of speech which we use today; but rather those used by the men of their times and countries. What those exactly were the commentator cannot determine as it were in advance, but only after a careful examination of the ancient literature of the East. The investigation, carried out, on this point, during the past forty or fifty years with greater care and diligence than ever before, has more clearly shown what forms of expression were used in those far off times, whether in poetic description or in the formulation of laws and rules of life or in recording the facts and events of history. The same inquiry has also shown the special pre-eminence of the people of Israel among all the other ancient nations of the East in their mode of compiling history, both by reason of its antiquity and by reasons of the faithful record of the events;

qualities which may well be attributed to the gift of divine inspiration and to the peculiar religious purpose of biblical history.

Appendix C

The Dogmatic Constitution Dei Verbum

Promulgated 18th November 1965

Chapter iii

Sacred Scripture, its inspiration and divine interpretation.

11. Those divinely revealed realities which are contained and presented in Sacred Scripture have been committed to writing under the inspiration of the Holy Spirit. For holy mother Church, relying on the belief of the Apostles (see John 20:31; 2 Tim. 3:16; 2 Peter 1:19-20, 3:15-16), holds that the books of both the Old and New Testaments in their entirety, with all their parts, are sacred and canonical because written under the inspiration of the Holy Spirit, they have God as their author and have been handed on as such to the Church herself. In composing the sacred books, God chose men and while employed by Him they made use of their powers and abilities, so that with Him acting in them and through them, they, as true authors, consigned to writing everything and only those things which He wanted.

Therefore, since everything asserted by the inspired authors or sacred writers must be held to be asserted by the Holy

Spirit, it follows that the books of Scripture must be acknowledged as teaching solidly, faithfully and without error that truth which God wanted put into sacred writings for the sake of salvation. Therefore "all Scripture is divinely inspired and has its use for teaching the truth and refuting error, for reformation of manners and discipline in right living, so that the man who belongs to God may be efficient and equipped for good work of every kind" (2 Tim. 3:16-17, Greek text).

12. However, since God speaks in Sacred Scripture through men in human fashion, the interpreter of Sacred Scripture, in order to see clearly what God wanted to communicate to us, should carefully investigate what meaning the sacred writers really intended, and what God wanted to manifest by means of their words.

To search out the intention of the sacred writers, attention should be given, among other things, to "literary forms." For truth is set forth and expressed differently in texts which are variously historical, prophetic, poetic, or of other forms of discourse. The interpreter must investigate what meaning the sacred writer intended to express and actually expressed in particular circumstances by using contemporary literary forms in accordance with the situation of his own time and culture. For the correct understanding of what the sacred author wanted to assert, due attention must be paid to the customary and characteristic styles of feeling, speaking and narrating which prevailed at the time of the sacred writer, and to the patterns men normally employed at that period in their everyday dealings with one another.

But, since Holy Scripture must be read and interpreted in the sacred spirit in which it was written, no less serious attention must be given to the content and unity of the whole of Scripture if the meaning of the sacred texts is to be correctly worked out. The living tradition of the whole Church must be taken into account along with the harmony which exists between elements of the faith. It is the task of exegetes to work according to these rules toward a better understanding and explanation of the meaning of Sacred Scripture, so that through preparatory study the judgment of the Church may mature. For all of what has been said about the way of interpreting Scripture is subject finally to the judgment of the Church, which carries out the divine commission and ministry of guarding and interpreting the word of God.

13. In Sacred Scripture, therefore, while the truth and holiness of God always remains intact, the marvellous "condescension" of eternal wisdom is clearly shown, "that we may learn the gentle kindness of God, which words cannot express, and how far He has gone in adapting His language with thoughtful concern for our weak human nature." For the words of God, expressed in human language, have been made like human discourse, just as the word of the eternal Father, when He took to Himself the flesh of human weakness, was in every way made like men.

CHAPTER IV
THE OLD TESTAMENT

14. In carefully planning and preparing the salvation of the whole human race the God of infinite love, by a special dispensation, chose for Himself a people to whom He would entrust His promises. First He entered into a covenant with Abraham (see Gen. 15:18) and, through Moses, with the people of Israel (see Ex. 24:8). To this people which He had acquired for Himself, He so manifested Himself through words and deeds as the one true and living God that Israel came to know by experience the ways of God with men. Then too, when God Himself spoke to them through the mouth of the prophets, Israel daily gained a deeper and clearer understanding of His ways and made them more widely known among the nations (see Ps. 21:29; 95:1-3; Is. 2:1-5; Jer. 3:17). The plan of salvation foretold by the sacred authors, recounted and explained by them, is found as the true word of God in the books of the Old Testament: these books, therefore, written under divine inspiration, remain permanently valuable. "For all that was written for our instruction, so that by steadfastness and the encouragement of the Scriptures we might have hope" (Rom. 15:4).

15. The principal purpose to which the plan of the old covenant was directed was to prepare for the coming of Christ, the redeemer of all and of the Messianic Kingdom, to announce this coming by prophecy (see Luke 24:44; John 5:39; 1 Peter 1:10), and to indicate its meaning through various types (see 1 Cor. 10:12).

Now the books of the Old Testament, in accordance with the state of mankind before the time of salvation established by Christ, reveal to all men the knowledge of God and of man and the ways in which God, just and merciful, deals with men. These books, though they also contain some things which are incomplete and temporary, nevertheless show us true divine pedagogy. These same books, then, give expression to a lively sense of God, contain a store of sublime teachings about God, sound wisdom about human life, and a wonderful treasury of prayers, and in them the mystery of our salvation is present in a hidden way. Christians should receive them with reverence.

16. God, the inspirer and author of both Testaments, wisely arranged that the New Testament be hidden in the Old and the Old be made manifest in the New. For, though Christ established the new covenant in His blood (see Luke 22:20; 1 Cor. 11:25), still the books of the Old Testament with all their parts, caught up into the proclamation of the Gospel, acquire and show forth their full meaning in the New Testament (see Matt. 5:17; Luke 24:27; Rom. 16:25-26; 2 Cor. 14:16) and in turn shed light on it and explain it.

The Old Testament

APPENDIX D

The Interpretation of the Bible in the Church

Pontifical Biblical Commission
23rd April, 1993

I. Methods and Approaches for Interpretation

A. Historical-Critical Method

The historical-critical method is the indispensable method for the scientific study of the meaning of ancient texts. Holy Scripture, inasmuch as it is the "word of God in human language," has been composed by human authors in all its various parts and in all the sources that lie behind them. Because of this, its proper understanding not only admits the use of this method but actually requires it.

1. History of the Method

For a correct understanding of this method as currently employed, a glance over its history will be of assistance. Certain

Appendix D – The Interpretation of Biblical Texts

elements of this method of interpretation are very ancient. They were used in antiquity by Greek commentators of classical literature and, much later, in the course of the patristic period by authors such as Origen, Jerome and Augustine. The method at that time was much less developed. Its modern forms are the result of refinements brought about especially since the time of the Renaissance humanists and their *recursus ad fontes* (return to the sources).

The textual criticism of the New Testament was able to be developed as a scientific discipline only from about 1800 onward, after its link with the *textus receptus* was severed. But the beginnings of literary criticism go back to the 17th century, to the work of Richard Simon, who drew attention to the doublets, discrepancies in content and differences of style observable in the Pentateuch-- discoveries not easy to reconcile with the attribution of the entire text to Moses as single author. In the 18th century, Jean Astruc was still satisfied that the matter could be explained on the basis that Moses had made use of various sources (especially two principal ones) to compose the Book of Genesis. But as time passed biblical critics contested the Mosaic authorship of the Pentateuch with ever growing confidence.

Literary criticism for a long time came to be identified with the attempt to distinguish in texts different sources. Thus it was that there developed in the 19th century the "documentary hypothesis," which sought to give an explanation of the editing of the Pentateuch. According to this hypothesis, four documents, to some extent parallel with each other, had been woven together:

that of the Yahwist (J), that of the Elohist (E), that of the Deuteronomist (D) and that of the priestly author (P); the final editor made use of this latter (priestly) document to provide a structure for the whole.

[…]

In the desire to establish the chronology of the biblical texts, this kind of literary criticism restricted itself to the task of dissecting and dismantling the text in order to identify the various sources. It did not pay sufficient attention to the final form of the biblical text and to the message which it conveyed in the state in which it actually exists (the contribution of editors was not held in high regard). This meant that historical-critical exegesis could often seem to be something which simply dissolved and destroyed the text. This was all the more the case when, under the influence of the comparative history of religions, such as it then was, or on the basis of certain philosophical ideas, some exegetes expressed highly negative judgments against the Bible.

It was Hermann Gunkel who brought the method out of the ghetto of literary criticism understood in this way. Although he continued to regard the books of the Pentateuch as compilations, he attended to the particular texture of the different elements of the text. He sought to define the genre of each piece (e.g., whether "legend" or "hymn") and its original setting in the life of the community or *Sitz im Leben* (e.g., a legal setting or a liturgical one, etc.).

Appendix D – The Interpretation of Biblical Texts

[…]

2. Principles

The fundamental principles of the historical-critical method in its classic form are the following:

It is a historical method, not only because it is applied to ancient texts--in this case, those of the Bible--and studies their significance from a historical point of view, but also and above all because it seeks to shed light upon the historical processes which gave rise to biblical texts, diachronic processes that were often complex and involved a long period of time. At the different stages of their production, the texts of the Bible were addressed to various categories of hearers or readers living in different places and different times.

It is a critical method, because in each of its steps (from textual criticism to redaction criticism) it operates with the help of scientific criteria that seek to be as objective as possible. In this way it aims to make accessible to the modern reader the meaning of biblical texts, often very difficult to comprehend.

As an analytical method, it studies the biblical text in the same fashion as it would study any other ancient text and comments upon it as an expression of human discourse. However, above all in the area of redaction criticism, it does allow the exegete to gain a better grasp of the content of divine revelation.

[…]

4. Evaluation

What value should we accord to the historical-critical method, especially at this present stage of its development?

It is a method which, when used in an objective manner, implies of itself no a priori. If its use is accompanied by a priori principles, that is not something pertaining to the method itself, but to certain hermeneutical choices which govern the interpretation and can be tendentious.

Oriented in its origins toward source criticism and the history of religions, the method has managed to provide fresh access to the Bible. It has shown the Bible to be a collection of writings, which most often, especially in the case of the Old Testament, are not the creation of a single author, but which have had a long prehistory inextricably tied either to the history of Israel or to that of the early church. Previously, the Jewish or Christian interpretation of the Bible had no clear awareness of the concrete and diverse historical conditions in which the word of God took root among the people; of all this it had only a general and remote awareness.

The early confrontation between traditional exegesis and the scientific approach, which initially consciously separated itself from faith and at times even opposed it, was assuredly painful; later however it proved to be salutary: once the method was freed from external prejudices, it led to a more precise understanding of the truth of sacred Scripture (cf. Dei Verbum, 12). According to Divino Afflante Spiritu, the search for the literal sense of

Scripture is an essential task of exegesis and, in order to fulfil this task, it is necessary to determine the literary genre of texts (cf. Enchiridion Biblicum, 560), something which the historical-critical method helps to achieve.

To be sure, the classic use of the historical-critical method reveals its limitations. It restricts itself to a search for the meaning of the biblical text within the historical circumstances that gave rise to it and is not concerned with other possibilities of meaning which have been revealed at later stages of the biblical revelation and history of the church. Nonetheless, this method has contributed to the production of works of exegesis and of biblical theology which are of great value.

For a long time now scholars have ceased combining the method with a philosophical system. More recently, there has been a tendency among exegetes to move the method in the direction of a greater insistence upon the form of a text, with less attention paid to its content. But this tendency has been corrected through the application of a more diversified semantics (the semantics of words, phrases, text) and through the study of the demands of the text from the point of view of action and life (aspect pragmatique).

With respect to the inclusion in the method of a synchronic analysis of texts, we must recognize that we are dealing here with a legitimate operation, for it is the text in its final stage, rather than in its earlier editions, which is the expression of the word of God. But diachronic study remains indispensable for making known the historical dynamism which animates sacred Scripture and for shedding light upon its rich complexity: For example, the covenant code (Ex. 21-23) reflects a political, social and religious situation of Israelite society different from that reflected in the other law codes preserved in Deuteronomy (Chapters 12-26) and in Leviticus (the holiness code, Chapters 17-26). We must take care not to replace the historicizing tendency, for which the older historical-critical exegesis is open to criticism, with the opposite excess, that of neglecting history in favour of an exegesis which would be exclusively synchronic.

To sum up, the goal of the historical-critical method is to determine, particularly in a diachronic manner, the meaning expressed by the biblical authors and editors. Along with other methods and approaches, the historical-critical method opens up to the modern reader a path to the meaning of the biblical text such as we have it today.